BENEATH THE S
T. S. O. L.

BY DAVID ENSMINGER

LEFT
OF THE
DIAL
BOOKS

THE VAULT LONG BEACH CA 2006 BY GREG MCWHORTER

T. S. O. L.

This project developed spontaneously and off-the-cuff after I interviewed Jack Grisham at Cactus Music in early November, 2018 when TSOL briefly toured Texas. I have been a devout fan since owning the prescient, groundbreaking "Weathered Statues" 7" EP in the mid-1980s; furthermore, for over twenty years, I have interviewed Grisham for various publications, plus at a punk round table (in front of members of Los Crudos/Limp Wrist and Pansy Division) at Modern Times Bookstore in San Francisco alongside underground music icons from Frightwig, the Nerves, the Dicks, and the Contractions. Grisham is such a rapid-fire and unharnessed speaker -- trenchantly funny and a demented punk court jester among the misfit cadres -- that I felt compelled to create this volume, which also taps into the archives of Welly, editor of longstanding Artcore zine, too. As you will note: some of the flyers document the Joe Wood-era of TSOL. I did that because, despite their glam-goth Hollywood Boulevard overtures, Change Today? remains popular, and I don't feel that era should be permanently buried. TSOL are survivors who have re-made themselves countless times; this book attempts to highlight, document, and lift the shadows just enough... to keep you wanting more.   David Ensminger, Nov. 24, 2018

Thanks to: Jack Grisham, Houston Press, PM Press, Cactus Music, Ed Colver (photos and cover photo), Jimmy Alvarado (flyers), Bijan Oskouie (photo & essay), Welly (transcription, design & interview) , Kyle Crutcher (flyers), Greg McWhorter (photos & flyers) & Kevin Murphy (photos).

PHOTO BY ED COLVER "The photograph I used for their 12" EP cover. I had a 12 1/4" X 12 1/4" night contrast stat print made, touched it up with black Sharpie and Whiteout and used 3" vinyl press Thor for the T.S.O.L. The major change I made was to take out the mic stand, since it appeared Jack was resting his pointed finger upon it."

WALK ALONE
THE MUSIC AND MAYHEM OF TSOL

TSOL will forever be the band that contorts punk's promise into a thousand shapes. Rising from the second-wave era of feral, clenched-fist, vitriolic, frenzied, panic-inducing greater Los Angeles-area punk, they quickly became avatars of aggressive, but artful, music. Their first two albums, 7", and EP have become essential-listening – a soundtrack to the teenage Western Front, the land of savage nights, music rules being blasted to bits, street-level politics, and deteriorating social milieus.

TSOL's music is filled to the brim with political rants; dark funereal musings fueled with spectral guitar; wild punk-ass binges; moody soliloquy-ridden song-poems about the human spirit enduring desperate times; evocations of fast cars and road-smeared kicks; plus tear-down-the-modes-of-control urges gleaned from piles of dog-eared philosophy books and tattered punk singles. Their home territory matters: they were molded by a surf-city, working class, reckless, and anti-authority upbringing in the same streets where skateboarders and hippies once scoured the dirty tides. To distant observers like me deeply influenced by the literary musing of "Weathered Statues" and the gasoline-binge of "Man and Machine," TSOL's turf was imagined as a panorama: miles of decrepit cemeteries, endless sloppy parties, gangland leather jacket terror, strip center conformity, and neighborhood meltdown. And TSOL was the pulsing soundtrack to turning this God-damn world upside down.

Many punk's shrugged off their progress, disdained the boys, or mutinied outright, when TSOL nurtured and expanded their musicality. Yet, they were ahead of the game. Bands like Youth Brigade (soon, the Brigade), Bad Religion, Code of Honor, and many more also morphed into concept-rock, to much less success. In the end, one can hear evidence, hints, and fault-lines of all sorts of new music, not just tattered punk chords and damaged screams, in the soundscape of TSOL ... Obviously, they were indebted to the Damned, but a listener can also glean bits of Joe Jackson, Magazine, Ultravox, early Boomtown Rats, Siouxsie and the Banshees and more. When stacked next to My War by Black Flag, Beneath the Shadows may seem suspect, but paired with 45 Grave, Gun Club, and especially bands like MIA and Mad Parade, it makes perfect sense.

Re-uniting in the dawn of the 2000s, they continued to offer morbid, dark dances and firepower, wicked glee and frontier style freedom. And, Jack

Grisham, as Walt Whitman said, contains multitudes -- he effortlessly fuses offhand philosophical introspection and wise-guy politico firebrand quips. Between the TSOL eras, he never skipped out of sight. Instead, he burrowed into the scene in bands like the obscure, synth-drenched, post-punk, danceable Cathedral of Tears; the more trad-rock Hollywood Blvd. darkness of Tender Fury (think of bands like Mary My Hope rather than Faster Pussycat); and the Joykiller, a tight unit well-admired by Flipside for their breakneck-speed, harmony-driven, streamlined sex-rock, which married 1990's punk with 1960's pop-a-delic undercurrents.

Though most fans zealously crave tunes like the grotesque revelry of "Blue Code," which practically invented the morbid-pop template for bands like Alkaline Trio, TSOL's misunderstood masterpiece Beneath The Shadows has aged well, especially side B, which contains their opus "Walk Away," which unfurls nightly at most of their gigs. But the deeper cuts from that vinyl slab, like the punishing guitar frenzy and circus-organ of "Other Side." remain blistering, while "Walk Alone" is their single greatest song that has not been marketed to the world. "Live in a world / Live in a world / of my own creation ... I walk alone," sings Jack, with complete fiery na-ked truth, while the skimmering, shattering guitar on "Waiting For You" is the perfect compliment to Jack's sonorous, stabbing voice. And, their chorus is seismic: "Tonight, tonight / I've been dreaming, dreaming of you" – each vowel carried on tumultuous electric winds.

To that end, Divided We Stand is also a partner to the same possibilities (sure, Disappear, Life, Liberty, and the Pursuit of Free Downloads, and the Trigger Complex are all tight, energized, and potent). "Sedative" at-tacks from the get-go, not unlike the Joykiller, and aims its gun scope at "accusations ... castration ... suffocation ... mutilation ... torn from society." In some way, the band comes full circle and still strikes out at the powers-that-be through the poetics of sharpened angst. "Serious" is a rock'n'roll vendetta against brainless protest, old men, senseless war, and more, which the band still plays with high-power thrust live coast to coast. "Fuck You Tough Guy" shreds machismo in two-minutes, and "See You Tomorrow" is a rhyme-heavy 1960's soul-punk venture. Meanwhile, the sedate, whispery "Loaded" is seductive, "Undressed" is a tight-paced disarming ode to bodily needs, "Being in Love" triggers a discussion about the disasters of romance, and "Happy" is a punchy, bubblegum, television theme show-esque slice of pop perfection.

That's what makes TSOL so undead – they are not static, inert, and fos-silized. They tremble with music, they whip up their own flames, they build bridges to both the past and future, and they are singular: they walk alone, damning the purists, setting fire to boilerplate punk clichés and fake turmoil (vs. their very own real struggles with addiction, marriage, and trend mongers), and living inside their own history, with a devil-knows wink and nod.

They cast the shadows, now, in which we all live and succumb.

HOUSTON 2011

JACK GRISHAM

ROCK'N'ROLL DECONTROL RELEASE PARTY: A SLIGHTLY EDITED CONVERSATION LIVE AT CACTUS MUSIC, HOUSTON, TX, NOVEMBER 9TH 2018

DAVID: So, TSOL actually have a new digital single ... and I want you to tell people about it because it surprised me, and I think it's gonna surprise you (the audience). It's kind of an interesting story -- it's a soul / hip hop kind of cover is that right?

JACK: I grew up with that stuff, which is funny because people go, "Oh, you must've listened to a ton of punk rock," but it's like I hardly ever listen to punk rock ... It's like if you're a plumber, you don't wanna go and sit around talking about pipes all day long, so I'd be dragging these hardcore guys to the shows. I'd go, "Oh, Curtis Mayfield's in town, we gotta go and see Curtis!" So, we'd be sitting there, and we saw Curtis, and it was great. We dragged all these hardcore guys down, and we were the only white guys there because it's downtown Long Beach. I don't know if any of you have been to Long Beach, but it was great because during "Freddi's Dead' they're doing the call and response, and I'm in heaven y'know, I'm just stoked. I dragged these guys to go and see Luther, y'know Luther Vandross, I dragged these guys all over the place. And it was funny because we'd go do ... I'm not proud of it ... maybe a robbery, and I'd have the Love Unlimited Orchestra on the 8-track. They're like, "Put on the Germs!" and I'm like, "Fuck the Germs, man, we've got Barry White!"
So, anyway, they'd always tease me about liking this shit. OK, I'll tell you a story, I was backstage at Luther Vandross one time, and it was so killer ... and everyone's looking at me like, "I have no idea who these people are who you enjoy but..." Anyway, I'm sitting there, and I'm in the orchestra pit, and Luther came out, and it's right when he did "Never Too Much" single, which is just great. So, I'm sitting there, and he starts to do "A House Is Not A Home," the Burt Bacharach song, and he walks up right in front of me, and Dionne Warwick is sitting in front of me, and she just stands up, and I'm like crying, actually tears in my eyes, and my buddy's going, "This is fucked, man." "No man, Luther, bitch."

... I'd always loved this stuff, so a friend of mine, well, this was fifteen years ago, said, "Hey, you should really check out this go-go beat that's going on in D.C. blah blah blah." So, I was checking out all these bands, and then this track came on, and I'm like, "This is bitching man because they're like real drums, it was like when everybody was using, well, I guess they still don't use real drums. So, I'm like, this is bitching, and we should cover this, and they go, "You're fucking whacked, we're not gonna be covering that."

It basically took me from 2005 until now to get them to agree to cover this song, and it's by Amerie and it's called "1 Thing". "It's this one thing that's got me tripping," right, and [the TSOL's guys] go, "What do you want to do? You want to speed it up?" And I'm like, "No, fuck that groove up? No way, we're not gonna... Let's just do it with hard guitars." So, we ended up covering this Amerie song called '1 Thing,' and the lyrics of the song are about her singing to a dude, saying, "Hey it's this thing that's got me tripping," y'know, "It's this 1 thing you did oh oh," and I'm like no man, it's like a kid singing to the government, saying, "Memories just keep ringing bells," like you been slippin', and we caught you trippin', man. Anyway, we covered it, and we just released it, but nobody knows it's out, well, you know it's out, but we just didn't want to tell anyone it was out yet.

DAVID: One thing I think it actually always goes back to is what a ground-breaking band you've always been, right? You introduced keyboards at a time when nobody was using keyboards...

AUDIENCE: It's the music police.

JACK: They're probably pissed off about my choice of covers. A lot of people weren't very happy about our decisions, but when I got into punk rock. I got into punk rock when I was a kid, and at the time, punk rock wasn't so much what you wore or what the band sounded like, it was all an attitude thing. So, you'd see a show, a literal show with Go Go's and Black Flag on the same bill y'know, and it wasn't ... no-one even had a problem with it. You'd go, "Who's playing tonight," and [someone would] go, "Oh, it's Wall Of Voodoo and the Germs." And so, Joan Jett's band the Blackhearts, the first time I saw them Joan wasn't singing. Who was singing was Carla Mad Dog from the Controllers. She was singing for the Blackhearts. So, you'd see all these cool, real open things man, and you'd be wide open to watching all this, and then later on it started getting, "Oh, it's this sound, and you've gotta do this, and you've gotta do that," and I always hated it.

It's like, no man, you've gotta be able to whatever you want to do and just have fun, and y'know, as later on as things progressed, I got treated better by some supposed non-punk bands than I got treated by punk bands. Like we just played... I might as well just talk shit, like I've ruined my career anyway (laughter). Someone said to me the other day, "Did you just get a tattoo on your face?" And I go, "Yeah," and they go "What about getting a job?" It's like, "I'm 57, where am I gonna work?" Anyway, I don't even know, I think I just lost my train of thought. Oh, I was looking for a song! And maybe OCD / ADD also have influenced our musical choices with this too. So, we just played this big show at home, and it was, 18,000 people in my backyard, so it was basically on the beach in front of my house, so it was great. I just ride my little scooter to this show. It was so trippy. So, here are all these supposed punk rock bands, and I felt like I was backstage at a Journey concert, y'know it's like, there was a special VIP areas backstage. [I] was like, "Whaddya mean, VIP, bitch? What are you do ... what is this?" Whatever...

AUDIENCE MEMBER: Very Important Punks.

JACK: Yeah, Very Important Punks, that is what it stands for. I'm gonna have to remember that next time I'm talking shit.

DAVID: I had to bring this up as it's the mid-term elections and it's the political season; you ran for Governor right?

JACK: Yeah, but just to bitch about healthcare.

DAVID: Was it in earnest, was it performance art, or were you really trying to make an impact on a certain issue?

JACK: It's funny now because now the bar is so low that I'm actually legitimate candidate (laughter). Back then Google me, and up pops up, well I'm sure this isn't the proper terminology these days, but y'know, you'd Google me, and I'm making out with a transvestite and I'm hammered y'know, but nowadays that's solid, and that's actually a positive I think for the platform (laughter) good for the platform, yeah you're right.

DAVID: Platform?

JACK: Yes, but then I was basically just bitching about healthcare. It's like we don't take care of our own people, and how is that a mark of a civilized society when we don't take care of our own? So, that's really what I was bitching about? (phone) Sorry.

DAVID: He's going to try and find this song and stream it for you live here right now.

JACK: I'm getting all these texts: "You're a son of a bitch, why don't you call me back?" "Why won't you answer your phone? Fuck you you're an asshole." This is what you get when you give your number out freely from the stage. You end up with thousands of text messages from angry kids that are upset about my music choices (plays new cover song). So, if you've never listened to Amerie you probably have no idea what this is right now.

DAVID: It doesn't sound a million miles away from your last few records, though. That's what's really compelling about it. It's not going to be jarring to people, y'know what I mean. I think back to like '82-'83 when you guys were stretching the boundaries out.

JACK: You know what that just reminded me of: John Cougar. Probably nobody in here likes John Cougar either, but I did hear a really cool story, when Prince's "Little Red Corvette" came out, John Cougar in the middle of a show, now I gotta fact check this, but I heard that he, in the middle of show, he stopped and played "Little Red Corvette." To the audience, he goes, "Hey you've gotta appreciate the song writing on this," and I thought that was really cool that he did that.

DAVID: Now I want to talk about the fact that people think that you're a Los Angeles band, you're one of the iconic bands of Los Angeles punk and hardcore, but you're actually a Long Beach band right? And how would you explain the difference to these people who've never been out there, between Long Beach and Los Angeles?

JACK: So, half of us came from Huntington Beach, half of us came from Long Beach. Long Beach was a Navy town, so I'm a Navy brat, like I used to have to salute my dad when he came home. "Jack Grisham reporting for inspection sir!" You can wonder why I've got a problem with authority, y'know what I'm saying ... Long Beach is like a Navy town, and then Huntington was like an oil workers surfer town is what it was. Like if you ever saw that show Maverick, I've got a great picture of me and Jack Kelly. Jack Kelly [Bart Maverick in the show] was the mayor of Huntington

Beach for a while, so it's a picture of me when I'm getting fucked up, and it's great. But L.A. was more like Arty, kind of like ... I don't know what to say, they were kinda like smaller and whatever. We're from the beach: big, tanned, crazy surf skate kids basically, and they didn't like us. They weren't very happy with us at all because they said it was violent and there were problems. If you get a chance, read John Doe's first book Under the Big Black Sun. It was nice because John let me have a chapter in there. He goes; "Hey Jack, can we get your opinion on this?" And I'm like, "Yeah, fuck you man." And y'know, I wrote this really angry letter, and he published it, which was really nice because John goes, "Hey that's my favorite chapter in the book." They were mad at us, but I think what they didn't understand is um, do you remember the PMRC was out and getting people about lyrics right? So, they're going, "Hey, these lyrics are damaging," and then all these whacked-out rock guys were going, "Our lyrics are just lyrics." Like well, wait a minute man, is the Bible just the Bible? Is the Constitution just the Constitution? It's like no: words inflame. We were reading all these French Existentialists, and taking it in, and then when these punks starting coming out, and I'm a kid and I'm hearing y'know, "Fuck the government, this, this, this." I'm going, "Yeah, yeah, yeah!" And then took that, and then put it on the streets, and acted like that. It was like a war, as far as we were concerned. It was a war against these people. So, when the cops came to a show to try to break up a punk rock show, we'd just pick up bottles and start throwing them and just go to war with them, and the older L.A. punks are going, "You're ruining our scene." It's like what? "Wait a minute man, you're like a bunch of freedom fighters bitching because the opposition took a tank to your clubhouse, you fucking big babies." It's like "We're in this man." ... I said, "You set these lyrics down, and then you're mad because I read what you wrote and believed it." ... the PMRC was right, they were totally right. Lyrics enflame, they change, they can hurt. I mean, later on, I got into neuro-linguistic programming and all that kinda crap, and you really realize the power of words. So, I told ... those guys, "Fuck you man, you started it, you made me like this." I remember telling Steve Jones that one time too. Steve Jones was pissed at me for something, I go "It's your fault bitch."

DAVID: Steve Jones of the Sex Pistols he's talking about.

JACK: Right, right. Yeah, the Sex Pistols. It's like my kids say to me all the time, it's like when I'm mad at them they go, "You raised us." And it was funny, I caught my daughter with some picture on Instagram. My youngest daughter, she's very attractive. They're both attractive, but they're out of control man. Anyway, so I saw this picture of my kids on Instagram, and I go, "Hey you gotta..." and she blocked me. Someone told me about the picture so I pretended I saw it. I go, "Hey... that picture's gotta go man, you're showing all this and this" and she goes, "How about this pops," they call me pops, "How about you just forget you even saw that fucking picture, and I'll try and forget about all that stuff that you've done that has scarred me for life."

CROWD: Laughter.

JACK: "You wanna talk about pictures, let's look at this!" "Alright, well..."

DAVID: One of my favourite stories about your kids is that when one of them was really really young, she came to a concert I think at the Troubadour, and she was like rolling around on the floor, and you were all happy because she's like rolling around the grime of rock'n'roll history...

CROWD: Laughter.

JACK: Yeah, well the first time my oldest kid, so I've got two daughters right, which is I guess if there's a deity, that's God's joke ... which I don't believe in anyway. But they're out of control, so my oldest daughter when she was fourteen, she goes; "I'm thinking of stage diving." I go, "I'll give you fifty bucks if you stage dive". She goes "I'm in," so she goes and flies off the stage, so of course I warned everyone there, "You grab a tit, you grab an ass -- you're gonna get it," so they were very cautious of her when she dove off. Then she comes up looking for her fifty, she goes she goes, "Where's my fifty?" I go, "Naw, no fifty, I would never trust an adult, fuck that."

CROWD: Laughter.

JACK: "There's no money on this!" And the littlest one's so funny ... I'd see her friends and they're all in little skirts, little whatever they're wearing, right. But one of them had on a T-shirt and a pair of jeans. We're playing this show, so I see this one in a T-shirt and a pair of jeans dive off right, and they're like fifteen at the time, sixteen, and dive off, and there's 1500 people going crazy, a bunch of punks. So, then I see the next one dive off and the next one dive off, and I'm tripping. I know I'm sober but this doesn't look right right? And what they were doing, there was a group of these girls, and one would dive off, and then they'd go to the bathroom and switch clothes. They had like one pair of jeans that these eight girls were switching off into to jump. So ... it was funny.

DAVID: ... You talk about how [lyrics] have meaning and insight ... all kinds of important issues. I'm just gonna come back to one ... that stuck in my mind, this lyric which I think fits the time, which is, "I love my country / but I hate my government." Is that a lyric you would stand by right now?

JACK: Yeah! I'm not a fan, I mean whatever. Nowadays saying that just sounds so "Let's go get donuts." I mean nobody's happy. But yeah, I'd still stand by it. I'm not a fan of anyone that wants to rule over another man. To me, that just seems really ridiculous. I wish they did government by lottery y'know, almost like Publishers Clearing House. Somebody shows up, "Sorry, but you're Senator this week."

CROWD: Laughter.

JACK: Y'know, the guys who want to do it shouldn't be doing it as far as I'm concerned. And when I ran for Governor, really, it was just to bitch healthcare in California, that's what it was so...

DAVID: ... when you listen to Jack when he's live in concert, the things he says between the songs are almost as important as the songs sometimes. And the rapport that you have and the antagonism you sometimes have with the audience, is kinda like Lenny Bruce. But it came into my mind on the live record from Long Beach actually, you talk about, "Hey we're all about to go to war and this time next year you're all gonna be dead in the desert from being drafted," and [the war is still happening years later], and it kinda blows your mind.

JACK: Yeah, especially our drummer. If anyone goes to the show tonight, our drummer Antonio that's playing with us, he did a year and a half in Baghdad, y'know and just listening to his stories, y'know PTSD ... can't throw pillows at him late at night.

CROWD: Nervous laughter.

JACK: Whatever... you can't grow up sometimes ... THEY'RE COMING! [he mimics throwing pillows at Antonio].

CROWD: Laughter.

JACK: Anyway, yeah horrific stories. Horrific. Terrible. Unbelievable. And it doesn't … the fact that the war … (sighs) … do we really wanna go here with this? I don't wanna sound like Biafra, fucking A. That's somebody that needs a spankin' that's for sure. Please stop Jello. Anyway, it doesn't take away their lack of courage or their bravery or … their actions, but the actual causes are … whatever.

DAVID: I want to go back to the idea of your relationship with the audience … some people get out there and just sing the song, they go through the soundtrack, they play like a jukebox, but you don't, you actively engage the audiences -- is it like every time you get up on that stage, it's like 'This is it,' like, 'This audience is what I live for right now'?

JACK: NO (laughter).

DAVID: Scratch that.

JACK: No, no I'm in, but we started playing backyard parties. Like when we started playing punk rock there wasn't really like a lot of clubs to do the gigs, so we'd play backyard parties. It'd be Black Flag and TSOL. One time we played to support a guy that was a Black Panther y'know, and he's got us playing in his living room. And so you'd be sitting there with all your friends. To me, it was never like, 'Oh this is an audience,' it's like "Hey, these are my friends, we like the same thing, we like the same music.' There's this connection. It's not like, "Hey I'm performing for you," it's like no, "I'm performing with you." It's like, "We're here to visit, to be here. Like enjoy each other, just have fun." I've always looked at shows like that. Where's it's like, "Hey, we're just here." Especially when we'd start playing because everybody would be hanging out, it's like "OK, Agent Orange is gonna play now," and everybody just basically … comes up and grabs an instrument, and somebody else comes up, and in-between everyone's sitting around and hanging out. Like the first time I really got stoked on punk rock was The Plugz, if you remember The Plugz. I love The Plugz.
So, The Plugz are playing in the Suburban Lawns house, right so … it's The Plugz and the Suburban Lawns at this house in Long Beach. So, I walk into the bedroom, by accident, y'know I'm some kid looking for whatever…

"jewelry" (laughter). Let's not get into that. But I walk in, there's The Plugz! The Plugz are all sitting there. And I'm like, because I don't know, because I hear what rock'n'roll supposed to be like, and the rock stars, and all this bullshit, and I walk in and I open the door and I go, "Oh, oh, sorry!" Because I've just entered the band's 'sanctum' y'know. I'm in there with that. And Barry (McBride) from The Plugz goes, "Oh, fuck it, have a beer kid," and I'm "oh my God, this is bitchin' man," and I was so stoked like on that, that there was nobody above anybody. It was real ... I know Socialism sometimes can be a dirty word, but if you really look at the true meaning of what we're talking about, it was really just ... guys hanging out, they're not better than you because they're in this band. They're not greater, it's your peers, it's your friends y'know. I've always looked at it like that.

And that's why I think this last show, when I walk in and this band that's supposedly a 'punk rock band' has their own special VIP area set-up back-stage that no-one's allowed to go in. And this other band has their own VIP area. And I'm just looking at them going, "You guys are just a fucking joke man." I mean it's ridiculous to me. It's like, but then you're hard on the re-cords, fuckin' great (laughter). Great, get hard. ... And they get bummed on me because I give phone numbers out all the time right? No-one ever wants to give me their phone number because I'll get a hold of it, and I'll just get on stage and go, "Oh, if you wanna call blah blah-blah, here's his number" (laughter). And sometimes I'll call on the mic. You know the only person who doesn't care if you give his number out? It's Keith Morris (phone rings), that's Keith bitching at me (laughter). And Keith always goes, "Jack you've been giving my number out again, huh?" (laughter) I love those calls. Fucking great Keith. Keith doesn't care, everyone else is crazy... I remember I got a call, I'm not going to say who it is...

AUDIENCE MEMBER: Aw, c'mon!

JACK: I can't, because I need 'em to do something for me, and I don't wan-na piss 'em off. I remember this band called, and we're playing a show. So, we're playing this show, and we get a phone call, and it's the book-ing...agent, and they go, "Hey, can you get these guys in the back, they don't wanna walk through the crowd?" And I'm like, "Are you fucking me, man? Seriously?" I go "Yeah, tell 'em I said to go fuck off, and I'm gonna let the crowd know that they're here and they didn't wanna walk through 'em." So, they didn't show up, they didn't go. It's crazy sometimes.

DAVID: At what point do you think that began to change, that sense of the egalitarian, that sense of 'we're all in it together,' that sense of breaking down the divide between audience and performer? At what stage do you remember that beginning to go away?

JACK: In the Nineties.

DAVID: In the Nineties?

JACK: It's like when punk rock got popular, that's when it got like that. When it's like, y'know it's crazy, it's like 'dude, I used to play house parties with you, what do you mean you've got security on you?' I mean I always had security, but they were fucking idiots from the neighborhood. I'll tell you one story, it's really funny ... you ever see that Norman Rockwell thing where the sailors got all the names tattooed on his arm all crossed off right. So, my buddy Dave went to prison in the Sixties and then got out in the Eighties. Like the early Eighties, so imagine that kind of brain damage going on right? And he's got all those names, girlfriend's names literally crossed off on his arm right? He comes to my house, and he's like bummed out. He goes "Jack, I heard you were a punk, that's not cool" (laughter). Because punk means you're gay right? He goes, "I know you did some shit man, but I was really bummed hearing that y'know." I go, "No ... What? ... C'mon man let me show you." "No, I don't wanna see what you do." I go "No, c'mon man, let me take you..." And I take him to this show, and it's TSOL playing in this park, right? And he pulls up, and he sees all these guys in black leather jackets (laughter). He was in like a big bike club, I'm not gonna say what bike club, but he was in a big bike club.

AUDIENCE MEMBER: Aw, c'mon.

JACK: Some things we can't say. Anyway, he goes "What's going on here?" He goes, "Where's all the fucking scooters?" I go, "What do you mean the scooters? This is punk rock!" He goes, "I don't get it, that guy's got leather on, what the fuck is going on?" He didn't know what was happening. And OK, and on the side of this, he had a dog with him. He had this Pitbull with him, his dog. So, he's got his dog with him, and we go to the show, and he's hanging out, saying, "This is alright, this is alright." So, the first band started playing, and the kids start slamming, and he's never seen it in his life, so he thinks it's a fight's breaking out, like, "What, oh, what the fuck?!" So, he lets the dog go out, and the dog is biting these kids. I go, "They're not fighting." Anyway, he's dead, he died of AIDS, but before he died I [took] him to a show with us. I was just busting Biafra's balls about something, so I take Dave to a show, he wanted to see a show, and TSOL at the time, we're getting 4 and 5,000 people at shows. It was crazy. So, we're playing a sold out Hollywood Palladium show, and I brought Dave there. So, Dave gets on stage in the middle of it, and he's got these bellbottom pants on, and they're all … well, he's been stepping on 'em, so there's a hole in the back, y'know what I mean? The bottom of the pants, and his hair's all down, and he's greasy, and he's kinda thin, and he gets the microphone, and he's hitting somebody that said something. He's hitting 'em with the microphone. And I'm sitting upstairs with Biafra, and Biafra goes, "Oh my god, who's this dinosaur, what the hell's happening?" "Oh, that's Dave." "He came with you?!" "Yeah, that's my neighbor, man, 'cmon!" Aw, fuck it was funny.

DAVID: I wanna talk about the fact that you were on Alternative Tentacles, you were also on Frontier…

JACK: We were on a different label every record. Like the Damned -- every record on a different label.

DAVID: So explain to these people, these good people, why that would happen.

JACK: Cuz we don't play well with others. And that's it. Signing contracts in blood. Because to me it was a joke. Like this whole thing was a joke. Like whoever thought people would like punk rock. Y'know what I mean? Nobody back then said, "Alright, I'm gonna get a band, and get a label, and get a tour bus, and we're gonna make millions of dollars." It's like, 'no,' they were making shitty little singles, y'know fucking off, and nobody cared. I was using different names all the time and signing contracts in blood and just screwing … one of our managers tried to get a record back that we had put out, and he asked for the original contract, and it's in blood. I signed it in blood, and he's going, "What the fuck is this? How am I gonna give this back?" "Just tell 'em I was incompetent … you're still incompetent!" Anyway … but nobody cared … c'mon nobody cared then y'know?

DAVID: Was it the same way with promoters? You talk about these huge shows. Like at the Olympic, there were thousands of kids at these shows … so obviously some people were taking it very seriously, and making money off it. Not you guys?

JACK: Well, it wasn't us.

DAVID: It was Goldenvoice.

JACK: Yeah … Well … when Goldenvoice first started, that's the big promoter out there, they do Coachella and everything now, but when that first started, it was a money laundering business for Gary Tovar. It was pot money, he was just trying to get rid of pot money. I remember Gibby (Butthole Surfers) asked me one time. We were out here, we're playing a show, and he goes, "I heard you made a bunch of money, how much money did you make?" I go, "Six thousand dollars from that show." Now, at the time, six thousand dollars is crazy money, it's like… that's like how much these guys make now. Not us, but somebody does. Other people make that. So, all it was, the reason we got paid that much money is because Gary was trying to launder pot money. And he actually got burned. I think he did ten years for it. So, he's paying all these bands this crazy money because he's just trying to move the money. And I remember once our manager goes, "Hey go to Tovar's house and pick up some weed, you gotta get some weed before the show." So, I went over there, and I'm hanging out with Tovar, and Tovar goes, and Vraney, Mike Vraney (Something Weird Video) our old manager, he's dead now too and he used to manage the Dead Kennedys. He died of cancer a while back y'know. Anyway, so Tovar goes, "Hey, Vraney said he needs some weed," he goes "here,'" and he give me this empty plastic bag, like a gallon bag right, and he goes, "Just go in the closet and just grab what you want," and there's a huge trash bag loaded with buds, so I just stuff it. It looked like a pillow. I made a big pillow out of it. And then I got home, and of course I pulled one bud out, put it in a little Ziploc bag, and went to our manager, and go, "Fuck, look at the buds he gave you, this is killer, this is killer.' But yeah, I know people did take it seriously, I just didn't. I kinda wish maybe I did. Sometimes when I was still living at my mom's 'til I was almost 40, I did wish that maybe I did take things a little more seriously. I think Leonard from The Dickies is the only one that's lived at his mother's longer than I did so…

DAVID: Well speaking of Gibby and the Butthole Surfers, I just put up a flyer of you guys playing in 1983 at the Lawndale Annex and you said 'oh my god, that's the show where you played saxophone for the band, so can you kinda spin that story, tell that story?

JACK: He just hit me up, he goes "hey can you play sax?" I'm like "oh yeah. Yeah". I couldn't but I don't think it mattered anyway, he didn't give a shit y'know so. He goes "alright let's go", and I'm like any y'know? Yeah, it was fun. We had a good time, that was fun.

DAVID: You talked about y'know these punk bands with these shitty singles, you guys almost entirely had EPs and LPs except for like "Weathered Statues," so why weren't you guys releasing like a thousand singles?

JACK: I don't know. We couldn't get it together. I mean that was the trouble with that band, it really was a punk band, at least for as long as I was in it. I know for a little while after I left they went and did something else for a while, but we just couldn't get it together. I used to tell people, "Look, if I could've went straight, I would've went straight." I tell people, "Know what my goal is? My goal would've been go to an Ivy League school, play sports and be in a fraternity." It's like, I tried (laughter). I can't even tell you how many times I tried. I'd get out of jail and go, "I'm going straight!" (laughter). "I'm a born again Christian today!' Y'know whatever it was, and then it was like Pinocchio, it's like I'd start off well, and then I'd run down the street and run into Lampwick and next thing you know I'm fucked up on Pleasure Island y'know.

DAVID: And your nose is this big.

JACK: How did this happen? How did I get in jail again? The plan was good, this was a good plan y'know.

DAVID: Well the other thing is I wanna ask you; do you think any movie at all, not a documentary, but even a fiction film, has ever actually caught the essence of the L.A. punk scene? Y'know there's Repo Man, there's Suburbia, there's all these films: do you think any of them even came close to capturing what it was really like?

JACK: Gangs Of New York. (laughter) Ow! Oh my god. (re-positions himself on the chair). I've got a screwed-up back. Yeah, I got an injury, argh my back (audience talks).

DAVID: Seriously, Gangs Of New York?

JACK: No, well that's kind of a joke. I screwed my back up a long time ago. OK, so we're playing the Ukrainian Culture Center with Flipper. It was TSOL and Flipper. And there was a rope, it was a big stage. There was rope hanging off the top of the stage, and it had like a noose, like my buddy had tied a noose, and he was trying to put it down over our drummer's head during the show right? So I got up, and I'm thinking I'm David Lee Roth or something, so I grab the rope. I'm way up, and I jump and swung off on this rope, and it went for a while and it just kept going, and it wasn't properly hand-tightened, so I'm head first, legs up in the air, and falling, and I, I may not have cat-like reflexes, I couldn't get my shit turned around, and I landed on my back on the piano and broke the legs (laughter) and just did it, and my back's been screwed. And I was black like a banana from my ass up to my neck, and the doctor says; "You're lucky you're not [paralyzed, that] you didn't snap your back".

AUDIENCE MEMBER: That was pretty cool man.

JACK: Yeah, well, it's not worth it when I can't lift the toilet seat in the morning, and I have to pee in the sink. So, recently, I just took another spill, so if you wanna see something funny... so Fletcher from Pennywise, you know Pennywise? Fletcher's a total idiot, and er, so he's drunk. I'm big, I'm weighing 300, and I'm not lying, normally I lie about that, but I'm telling you the truth ... I'm actually gonna sue United Airlines, but that's a whole other story. I was on the plane, and the stewardess - flight attendant - bumped into me, and I go "Woah," and she goes, "Be glad I'm not 300 pounds." "I'm fucking 300, what do you mean you're not 300? What does that mean?" So, I'm gonna call United and try and get some free flights. "I'm a person of size who feels discriminated against' (laughter). Anyway, that's a whole other issue, but we're playing this show. I'm 300, Fletcher's like 340, and we're playing this show at this club by my house called The Observatory. It's a great place, 1,500 people, and they don't care how many people we put on the guest list, so we have 300 people guest listed on top of that. All the neighborhood comes out. It's a blast right? So, it's stage, and then there's six feet of open space like, from you to that stage, open space, and then the crowd, right? So, I'm up there playing, and Fletcher's all drunk, and he grabs me, and he puts his arms around me, and in his drunken mind, he thinks that somehow we're going to -- six hundred and forty pounds of fat, white, man ass -- is somehow gonna fly over the barricade, and I guess land onto the waiting arms of a fifteen or sixteen year old girl, who's going to squire us around the dance floor before setting us down on the side (laughter).

Well yeah, in a drunken mind, that's what it is. He grabbed me, and we basically went head first into the concrete just like this. Two fat guys just going over, and he, because he had my arms wrapped I was going head first, onto the concrete, with him on top of me, and luckily I just twisted my back a little bit, and I just hit my shoulder, dusted my shoulder, dusted my back, same thing. And it was funny, my cardiologist called me, and he goes, because they'd just taken me off blood thinners -- I'm on blood thinners, I'm 57, luckily I can get an erection still (laughter) – anyway, so my cardiologist called, and goes, "Thank god you're off those blood thinners. That would've been a catastrophic act. I was watching that on YouTube" (laughter). Killer, anyway, so now ... it went out again a couple of days ago, and it's just killing me, so I twist every once in a while, and it feels like somebody just stabbed me.

DAVID: I wanna open it up the audience now. This is your one big chance, Jack does not do this stuff often, right? Usually, you just play the show, you don't come hang out with...

JACK: Well, I do, but I'm usually at home alone, and I ask myself the questions (laughter), and the usual answer is I have no fucking idea. "Why did ya' get married again?" "I have no fucking idea." Married three times, only divorced once.

DAVID: So, is there something we'd like to ask our favorite idol here? Anyone got a question?

JACK: No, he was waving away a fly.

DAVID: You haven't got a question, just waving, how about you?

AUDIENCE MEMBER: What was the studio set-up like on Alternative Tentacles?

JACK: There wasn't a studio. So, Alternative Tentacles, that was Jello's label, and the reason why we even ended up on there is because our manager, Mike Vraney, also managed the Dead Kennedys, so we ended up doing that. But they let us record wherever we wanted.
AUDIENCE MEMBER: And that could've been in somebody's house?

JACK: Anywhere. Wherever you're at, somebody, wherever you're gonna record. Thom Wilson, who was the producer that produced all the TSOL records, was well liked in a lot of studios in L.A., so he got us in good places, we were actually.

AUDIENCE MEMBER: Dance With Me and Beneath The Shadows are really good quality.

JACK: Well, ... it's funny ... our first EP was only seven minutes ... so I don't know exactly, you know, Google it. Anyway, it was around seven minutes. That was recorded in an afternoon. It was five hours, and you can actually hear a motorcycle go by on one of the songs because I was doing vocals in the bathroom, and Dance With Me, our second record, was recorded in sixteen hours. It was two eight hour days, and we just went in, and the cool thing is, Thom Wilson just let us do whatever we wanted. He was so cool. Like ... these punk bands ... he didn't try to produce 'em ... he didn't worry about anything, like sometimes now I'll go back to listen to those records and[feel] "Oh my god, man." But he would just let it go, like if we were off time or something was a little out of tune, or I was way flat, he didn't care. He just said, "Hey, I just wanna get a picture of you guys being you guys." And he didn't care, like he really ... loved punk rock, and he just wanted to capture it as it was. Like he didn't try to make it, y'know, better, or better produced or anything. He said, " ... I just want a snapshot of what you guys are doing." There's even a song on ... I think the Weathered Statues single ... where I'm laughing in the song, but the laugh wasn't there on purpose, it was just because I had the lyrics in my hand. I'd never done it, and it was so fast -- "Inewoawcarwaaargh!" And Thom goes; "We got it, first take" (laughter). "Wait a minute!" [I said]. "No, we got it, first take." (laughter). And he just left it, he didn't care.

DAVID: You can ... purely document that way.

JACK: Yeah, and Thom, sadly, Thom died too, so he's gone. And it's weird being alive with all these guys ... dying. It's strange, I didn't think I'd be this old, I never thought I'd be this old ... that bullshit about ...

DAVID: Live fast, die young?

JACK: Yeah, didn't happen for a lot of us. I'm my father's age now, which is strange. I hope my dad wasn't doing shit like I'm doing now. It really creeps out man, it's like. I will tell ya, I can say this funny porn story. My dad was total Navy, hardcore Navy, like really ... really strict. ... my taste had expanded by that time, and there was no internet, so I had a magazine. I had a magazine and I had left it in the bathroom, and it was transvestites with whips. It was a connoisseur's magazine (laughter). So, my grandmother had Alzheimer's ... so I guess I forgot the magazine in the bathroom, and my grandmother grabbed it. And she was walking around with it, and my dad's like, "Hey, Gigi whaddya got?" (laughter) He looks at it right, and I remember, I'm sitting in the living room watching cartoons, and my dad walks up, and he tosses it on my lap, and he goes, "Gigi had your trash" (laughter). C'mon dad, I'm pretty much a straight man.

DAVID: Pretty much.

JACK: Pretty much, and my dad, it's funny because my dad ... I'd wear dresses all the time, and he would just bum out. He liked it when I got my head shaved until he found out why I shaved my head. Because I didn't want people grabbing my hair in fight, so I kept my head shaved and greased. And I'd wear these dresses, and one night I got out, and I got beaten pretty bad. I had lumps all over me, y'know, two black eyes and my ribs had been kicked. We got in a scuffle with these guys, these hippies, at a party. I mean they're not real hippies, they were more like greaser hippies. And, anyway, it was me and a buddy, and we took a pretty bad beating, so the next morning I'm wearing this bitchin' Japanese dress I had. So, I'm sitting in the room, watching cartoons, eating my cereal, and I got my earrings on, and I'm wearing this Japanese dress and eating with the black eyes, and my dad comes ... oh god, my dad walks downstairs, he sees me, and he goes, "Alright, you finally got your fucking ass kicked" (laughter). "It took fifteen to do it, old man" (laughter). But when you have a dad like that, it's crazy because ... you have a real problem with authority. After that, OK, one more quick story I'll tell ya, sorry about this, but... I'll give you the other side of it also.

I got my two kids in the car, and my daughter at the time is a skinhead, anarchy punk, my oldest one, y'know she's got the anarchy patch on her, the whole thing. And I'm looking at the surf in the morning, and the girl, the woman I was married to at the time was really rough, she was rough. And um, so it's early, and I'm supposed to be getting the kids to school, and I'm checking the surf, and I realize I'm late. I start driving home, and I'm splitting, so of course I get red-lighted right? I'm thinking, "I've got the cop red-lighting me, or I got the wife at home who's gonna yell at me," so I'm like, I'm just gonna go home. Right, I'm gonna go home, so I decide I'm not gonna pull over (laughter). My daughter's in there, she's got her head shaved, y'know, her green army jacket, the anarchy thing, and she goes, "Dad the cops are behind you," and I go "Yeah, fuck him." And that point, she realized that the anarchy patch on her jacket was cloth, and her father was the real thing (laughter). So, the craziest part about this story is, he follows me, it's about a mile and a half, almost two miles to my house, and I'm not pulling over, and he's (siren sound three times), y'know, when they do that when you don't pull over. It goes to that sound. So, I pull up at the house, and he gets off, he's on a motorcycle, and he gets off, and he comes up to the window and goes, "Hey, I'm trying to..." And I go " ... Look, hey buddy, I think I gotta tail light out back there, why don't you check that out?" I go, "Annie, get in there, get your sister, get her cleaned up, get her ready for school." The guy's like yelling at me, so I get out, and I'm like smart assin', y'know it's like I've lost it, I'm smart assin', and he writes me up for everything he can possibly write me up for. Okay, great. So, I get in the house, and I'm pissed off, and after a couple of minutes of getting in the house I think, y'know what, you were a fucking asshole man. Like I'm looking at my house thinking I'm an asshole. I'm thinking I'm gonna have to go up to the police station and apologize to that guy. I think about it ... a quick amends for me is not always so quick.

I think about it for about two weeks, and I'm walking down the bike path, and I'm with my wife, and I see him sitting on his motorcycle, right? And I go. "Oh it's him, it's him, I go I gotta go clean this up." My wife's going, "You sure?" I go, "Yeah, I'm going," right. I start walking up, and he sees me, and he gets off the bike and he covers the holster, and he goes, "Alright, stop right there," and he puts his hand out because he thinks I'm coming in for round two right? And I walk up and I say, "Hey look, I'm sorry." I go, "I just wanna tell you that I'm sorry, you didn't deserve to be treated like that." I go, 'You're out here just doing a job, and you don't need some asshole like me fucking with you in the morning when you're just trying to do your job, here in the community, and I just wanna tell you how sorry I am for the way that I treated you." And I started to walk away, and he goes, "Hey, wait a minute man," he goes "Wait a minute." And he takes his glasses off, and he's crying, he's got like a tear in his eye, and he sticks his hand out, he goes, "Hey ... twenty years on the force and that's the first time anybody's ever apologized to me." So, it was cool, and we shook hands, and it's funny. Now, it's like in my neighborhood, they joke about me being the mayor, but y'know everybody -- the police, everybody -- is stoked. They're all nice, they like to see me, but then he was just doing his job, and y'know what's funny, if you go back and look at this stuff, the police were supposed to be our militia. I don't know if you're aware of that, but that was our militia against the government, the local police, but somehow we got away from that. I remind 'em that every time I talk to 'em (laughter), "It's you and me against these guys."

DAVID: I forgot to mention: you're quite the photographer, and where exactly does that come from?

JACK: Shoot, if you ever get on Instagram, you need to look, it's jackgrishamphoto. I shoot people. I have trouble having connections with people, so I found that through a camera I can actually get close to people. But the way I got started doing it, I was posing ... I'd go with these magazine guys, we'd have to go shoot for a magazine or whatever. And I fucking hated it. But I ran into a lot of these great photographers. And so one time out of the blue I get this message from this photographer, and he's shot in Rolling Stone and all these magazines, and it's an email from him, and I hadn't shot with him in fifteen years. And he wrote me, he said, "Jack, I download stuff off the internet for inspiration," and he goes, "And six of the last ten things I downloaded came off your phone, why don't you buy a fucking camera?" (laughter) That was the whole email, and then so I started shooting people after that. And y'know, the cool thing is I'm involved in the recovery community. I've been clean and sober for almost thirty years. So, twenty-nine years and nine months.

The one good thing I've been able to do is, I've been able to shoot a lot of people with injuries. For some reason, it's therapeutic. I shoot a lot of people who are afraid to see themselves. They're scared, like maybe a lot of women, y'know with mastectomies, cancer issues, and other issues. So, I shoot 'em, so they can see how they really look. And I don't use filters, and I don't take stuff off. I think women are beautiful as they are. I like it. I really ... I'm a fan of women. Like I tell some of these photographers, "You don't even like women, why do you fucking shoot 'em dude? You turn 'em into these monsters with no flesh on 'em." So, it's been really bitching to be able to sit with these people and shoot 'em, and I get great emails from them saying, "Hey, it really helped me to go back to work, y'know show up." And they just did a story ... I shot a women the other day because they're doing a story on it in the local magazine. It's this woman like coming to terms with getting older, so she wanted me to shoot her, so she could see what she looks like basically through someone else's eyes, without make-up, without anything, just being her. And she's writing about her experience of it for a local magazine.

DAVID: And it seems to me in a way it is sort of very punk rock, right? It's unadorned, it's straight forward, it is unembellished, right?

JACK: Right, and the same thing, sometimes I get these actors and actresses, and people who want me to shoot 'em. And they say, "Well, come up to L.A. and we're gonna rent you a studio, we'll get it set up." I go, "Fuck that, put 'em in a car and have 'em drive to my garage." (laughter). I shoot in my garage, and I just shot this Tony winning actress a couple of weeks ago, and it was funny because she actually was willing to come down. And I told her, and she's older, and she's in her seventies, and I said, "Hey, you know this is gonna be unvarnished, you're aware of that?" And she goes, "Yeah, I'm in, I'm in." So, it was cool. She came and sat in the garage with me ... just me and her, and we just shot. It was great.

DAVID: So do we have any other questions out there? Anyone else wanna? This is it man, it doesn't come around too often. Anybody?

AUDIENCE MEMBER: Do you have any vinyls?

JACK: I don't have vinyl, I don't have anything.

DAVID: And he sold out of his damn book.

JACK: I don't have any books, I don't have any vinyl, I don't have nothing. I just came to visit.

DAVID: Well do check him out, he's got American Demon and another too, so get online, check 'em out, they're fantastic.

AUDIENCE MEMBER: How did you discover punk rock?

JACK: Well, I my brother-in-law was from England. So, when the Sex Pistols first came out ... and then when we had Rodney on the ROQ, and Rodney used to do his Sunday show. So, that's how I started getting into it. And, at first, it tripped me out, like why are these people dressing and looking like this? Like I didn't understand why music would make somebody do something like that. It reminded me of like the guys in Grease, dressed like fifties rockers. That always fucked me up like, "Really? You dress like that for that music?" Y'know, I didn't get it. I dressed like I did for surfing, so I'm not the smartest block out there. Yeah? Sorry...

AUDIENCE MEMBER: So, punk rock has a major influence in hip hop as well, in hip hop culture: what was your initial thought when a lot of hip hop artists were coming out, dressing like punk rock, and adopting a lot of punk rock music?

JACK: Well I loved a lot of the hip hop stuff because one of my friends played keyboards for like Eazy-E, Mellow Man Ace, and Kid Frost...

AUDIENCE MEMBER: Wow!

JACK: So I go and hang out, and they were, I'll tell you a fucking, er is anybody related to, um what's the guy's name from Creedence? John Fogerty. Nobody. Does anyone care?

AUDIENCE: Laughter.

JACK: I don't wanna get my ass kicked.

DAVID: Ah, I love Creedence.

JACK: Right, so anyway, I went to the same Junior High as Snoop Dogg, so we went to the same junior high school together, so we were actually recording, and Snoop and his guys were there, and we there, so we're playing basketball in-between the sessions at this secluded recording place, right? So, then the door opens and this blue convertible, this Corvette, pulls up and parks right under the fucking hoop, like right under the hoop right, and John Forgery gets out. And I go, "Hey dude, we're fucking shooting man." And one of Snoop's guys goes, "Take it easy, that's Creedence." I go, "Fuck Creedence, man, he's right under the fucking basket."

AUDIENCE: Laughter.

JACK: Cuz y'know, coming from punk rock. Like they're all stoked, "It's Creedence man.' So, anyway, I took my pants off and just dropped my business all over his car. Like on the hood...
AUDIENCE: Laughter and applause.

JACK: And it was funny cause they're going "Aw, that's cold man." I'm like, "Fuck him, we're in the middle of a game, I'm shooting man." Anyway, whatever it was pretty funny. Especially when he came out and opened his door handle and rubbed this...

AUDIENCE: Laughter.

JACK: So, I feel pretty good about that. I mean I'll apologize if I see him if I feel bad.

DAVID: I've got a photo down here of the singer of Fishbone, and I was wondering, do you see Fishbone as ... a halfway point between funk / hip hop and punk?

JACK: Angelo's great. The best. I'll tell you the best front man, Angelo was one of them, I tell them all the time when I see 'em, it's like "Ah, dude you're the best." John Denney from the Weirdos and Angelo, they were the best. They're the best frontmen out of L.A., ever. They were great. Still great, bitchin'. I'm actually supposed to shoot him, but we haven't got a chance to put it together.

DAVID: Another question before we go?

AUDIENCE MEMBER: So, that movie that came out in the 1980s, Suburbia. How did those bands end up in it -- was it an actual show and they came to record it?

JACK: Nah, it wasn't a real show.

AUDIENCE MEMBER: Did you get paid and shit? Like what happened, how did y'all end up there?

JACK: Well, I think they just asked us to do it. Penelope just asked us to do it. And what's sad, it's actually like a little embarrassing for me because I didn't have any idea that they were really making a movie. Like my ego was so out of check that like I had no idea [it was] a movie. Like if you're that far gone ... Like they're shooting a movie... so in the scene, if you watch Suburbia, I'm going like this (finger across throat), I'm telling the director to cut. It wasn't like cut the music, it's like, "No, cut those cameras." That's how out of it I was. Like not even realizing that it was movie, that they're making a movie. This is how my ego got way out of hand. Thankfully, it got smashed. You wouldn't think so, but it did.

FRIDAY SEPT. 7

THE DILS CONTRACT

THE DILS KILL CAT

SAT. SEPT. 22 CRIM

WEIRI

SAT. SEPT. 29 go go

SPECIAL GUEST

MUTANTS
X

1839 GEARY

S.F. AT FILL

WEIRDOS

Hollywood/ Los Angeles

INK SECTION

OUCHTONES SAT. AUG. 25th

39 GEARY St.

S.F. AT FILLMORE

9:00

EPT 1st. Sat

UXEDOMOON

LEVI AND THE ROCKATS

LEVI AND THE ROCKATS

DA,

works lik
reconcep-
to build
's con-
ver-

TURDAY

SEPT. 8 the DILS

THE VAULT LONG BEACH CA 2006 BY GREG MCWHORTER

NOT-SO-SILENT SCREAMS!
TSOL AT WALTERS SATURDAY MAY 7
ORIGINALLY APPEARED IN HOUSTON PRESS, MAY 2011

In the dramatic, razor-sharpened lens of TSOL songs, suburbia is far from a sleepy wonderland bedecked with slick malls and coiffured lawns. Those tracts of same-samey homes are chock-full of demons, such as singer Grisham himself, who wandered the bland wasteland of the American dream in the early 1980s like a priest of peril to the lost boys, misfits, and rebels.

With the musical heft, prowess, and punk-gone-Goth shadings of the band backing him throughout these treacherous territories, Grisham always projects a persona that seems like a large amalgam: he's a Lenny Bruce style iconoclast, a suave but demented Chris Isaak, and a nihilist vis-à-vis The Joker (Batman), not to mention a mouthy raconteur who can easily stir stories about Tesco Vee (The Meatmen), Black Panthers, and unemployment between jokes on stage.

Starting in 1980, TSOL pushed aside the art school cadres that shaped new music in Southern California, injecting big doses of Huntington Beach hormones into punk rock. Like Agent Orange and Social Distortion, though, they didn't succumb to the choleric "fast and lean" rules of homogenized hardcore. Having soaked up earlier waves of bands like the Germs, they favored something more poetic and fertile.

After imploding after just a handful of years, Grisham steered bands such as Cathedral of Tears, Tender Fury, and the Joykiller, but the reformed TSOL, who have seized the last decade with a hard grip, have remained invigorating and promising, delivering worthy music just as punks from their own generation, like Keith Morris and Mike Watt, chisel and hone their own late-period ruckus too. Both periods, new and old, of TSOL melted into a fierce onslaught on Saturday at Walters on Washington.

Since the beginning of TSOL, Grisham could deftly balance anti-political countercultural harangues ("Abolish Government/Silent Majority") with narrative structures more reminiscent of 19th century masters like Edgar Allen Poe and Bram Stoker on songs like "Silent Scream." Like a poet of the macabre, he was a man of letters in a nest of shaven-haired punk vipers. Grisham aimed for the murky, allegorical, and dense, weaving the lore of literature into his own memory as a wicked outsider in the land of sun and fun. To listen to the TSOL is to feel his breath, both cold and vitriolic, causing creepy crawls down one's spine in the vein of "Code Blue," which the band whips out as the last goodbye nearly every show.

TSOL still explores the pent-up angst and alienation lurking in the male psyche, including the minefields of sexuality and personal power at odds with control, whose dimensions feel like a Kafka novel. They abundantly revealed this Saturday, giving the crowd quick gulps of the veteran tune "I'm Tired," with its angry retorts against the "system" and "process" that prey on those "who don't listen." Those same tremors occur decades later in "Terrible People" as well, released early 2000s, which they pummeled the crowd with early on in the set. In that tune, suburban moms dote on children that are no more than "rats in the system," and people are still not listening, according to Grisham, as they generate "monsters and victims."

These same concerns get more articulate throughout later TSOL, who gained a powerful foothold during the 2000s. This older, wiser version eschews some of the woozy, hallmark poesy of their earlier days, replacing it with buckets of brio and rage. The band newly focused their anti-authority sentiments in an era of Bush's endless wars in tunes like "Serious," which popped up near the end of the set: "Let's make a bomb before feeding our children... vote what you want, the monster is replaced ... love your country, hate your government." Likewise, songs like "Fuck You Tough Guy," also unleashed from the same album ("Divided We Stand"), offered no respite from the iconoclasm as well. "No teachers, no parents, no classrooms ... no idols," they sung, older at heart, but with no less rancor towards the forces that dealt them blows years before.

Punk rock has always been a call to arms for such freedom seekers, marginalized youth, artful demons, and queer/queered people, just like it has always been saturated with uncontrolled ideas and bodies, which writhed all night to tunes like "Dance with Me," a soundtrack to "convulsions" and "demonic beats" that made the crowd revisit 1982. Sure, the Dead Boys and New York Dolls might have faded by then, but Grisham embodied a hybrid between such rebels and the beachcore troops. He was the linebacker-built, rakish guy unleashing motorcycle boots with razor-sharp spurs on idiots who dared cross him, but he also worked the stage with theatrical flare just as the band supplemented their trademark bracing, fissured guitar with keyboards and strings, breaking hardcore codes. Unlike some previous tours, those extra musical elements were AWOL during the set this past weekend.

TSOL might have emerged as byproducts of the decline and fall of the 1970s - the flops of the Me Generation – but they still recognize and invoke a breeding ground of despair. Some in the audience know this too well, recognizing their own dark memories mirrored in Grisham's potent narratives. His politics and vehemence may seem fringe to some, while others consider his songs too turgid.

Yet, Grisham is still an impenetrable mystery that commands the stage like a Rottweiler treading back and forth. As an undaunted, mad, and dashing culprit, he worked the small space with endless gusto, holding forth like a tribal elder of the reckless and ribald. Though he no longer dons white-face or other make-up, he still invokes the sexual deviance of early Adam Ant, the vampire intelligence and wit of Dave Vanian (The Damned), the Hollywood shit-grin of Eric Draven (The Crow), and becomes a larger than life male Siouxsie Sioux. That is, he really can sing, not just spit out the words with a blast furnace mouth.

Grisham is not bolted to that nostalgia, or anyone's preconceived notions of what constitutes the living heritage of punk, as he noted to me while crammed in the van after the delirious show. Years back, restless people like him wrote on the back of punk flyers not Tweets, made shirts chockfull of zippers that went nowhere, and wore bright yellow jackets emblazoned with anarchy signs for a cruise down the block, causing neighbors to slam windows shut. Those were the days, though, chronicled in his just released memoir An American Demon, that included disappearing from his family as early as age 11, enduring an intensely incendiary climate while fronting his pre-TSOL band Vicious Circle (when people bombed his car, forcing him into Alaskan exile), and being on the 'sauce' -- blurring the years with alcohol.

On Saturday, the band behind him, minus original bass player Mike Roche, never missed a single seismic beat, even as they were sweat-drenched and rammed frequently by the invasive, riotous crowd. As the band struck their chords well beyond the pale midnight hour, Grisham briefly became the Lord of the Flies. The audience danced with him, burning away the last cinders of their cocoons, freeing themselves in the humid and bleary night, letting TSOL's songs linger in their hearts and minds, like truths summed up in their gashed heads and torn clothes. But as the night closed, that same man hoped to lead them towards seizing the day, not disappearing into the black hole of social decay. And that he did.

JACK GRISHAM (SINGER) AND RON EMORY (GUITARIST) OF TSOL

Jack Grisham, singer of beach boys gone berserk TSOL, is a tour-de-force of American punk history still operating in full-bore style. His memoir An American Demon, which surveys his cataclysmic youth and early career, is not for the timid and meek. Like a meld of Oscar Wilde's Dorian Gray with Fight Club and Clockwork Orange, he offers a savage poetry with an undertow of wit. In his lens, not-so-quiet Los Angeles suburbs become awash with dysfunction, revolt, and violence. Yet, in the end he offers a sense of recovery as well, a way to transcend personal chaos and find solace in the lurking memories. This was originally published in both the zine Left of the Dial and the book Left of the Dial (PM Press).

How is touring different in 2001 compared to 1982?

Jack: I don't want to jinx it (laughs). It was a little more out there then. They weren't that hip to the way you looked, you know what I mean? It was a definite freak show, not even necessarily being punk, if you got out of your vehicle with a dress on people were bummed. Now you walk into truck stops and you don't have to fight someone.

Do you prefer a show when you stop into town by yourself, or the package tours like Social Chaos and Warped?

Jack: Sometimes it's fun to go with your friends. You have more people to fuck around with. We all hang out. Sometimes in those groups with a bunch of bands you're friends with everyone, and you fuck around all day, like you switch cars and ride with another group of guys or whatever. It makes it kinda fun.

Supposedly on the Warped tour, you guys were the oldest, but the most obnoxious?

Jack: We were threatened with getting kicked off the tour. It was stupid because it wasn't even a big deal. We were getting caught for chewing gum and lying, you know? It wasn't like we were doing anything fucked, but I was kinda bummed. We were kidnapping kids -- that was our deal. We were kidnapping kids, and then we'd keep them with us for three or four days, right? And now I hear that Pennywise is doing that, it's like Survivor with Pennywise, and now everyone is going to be saying, "Man, Pennywise is kidnapping kids."

You've said that punk has been turned into a Sprite commercial, but what could have been done to prevent that?

People not selling shit out.

Meaning?

People not wanting to make money off the stuff. I don't blame them. There were always guys who were just punks, and guys who were trying to make money off of them. Like I remember guys going, "Hey man, I'm making splatter shirts." Remember splatter shirts Ron, what was that guy's name? Somebody would come up with a scam, like hey we're making splatter shirts, and it was kinda a cool thing, so people started cashing in on it. But there were people who were doing things and not cashing in on it...

You've compared yourselves to the old blues musicians who got ripped off by the white 1950's rock n rollers.

Jack: Still do. Yeah, because we were stupid and didn't care. To us, it wasn't a business. We weren't making shrewd business decisions, we were like, "Give us a couple six packs of beer and a pen and we'll sign."

Ron: With our first record it was like, "Record contract? Okay, whatever."

Jack: If you look back at our early contracts, they're signed in blood. It was like, hey, watch this. We'd throw contracts down the toilet and say we didn't care. We didn't understand anything about the business, we never had a lawyer, we didn't ask about publishing, we had nothing, and they took everything.

Do you think a lot of bands, especially over the last ten years, use the tag punk to legitimize music that is basically really mediocre and faceless?

Jack: Yeah, because a lot of it is not what you would call punk rock. When we started out, Elvis Costello was punk. I mean the Go-Go's were punk. There was a lot of stuff like that, which was considered punk rock. It was different because back then it was in the attitude, instead of the music. I mean the music was cutting edge or whatever, more experimental, but it was mainly the attitude. Now, there's the music and the look, but there's no attitude to it. There's nothing that truly makes it punk rock.

What happened in the evolution of punk and hardcore that made it eventually become so rigid it terms of the look, sound, and feel?

Jack: It started getting bigger.

But at the same time, TSOL expanded its song structures and started using keyboards.

Jack: A lot of it was people who thought they knew what it was, you know what I'm saying? They thought they knew what it was, so they started copying these people. When we first started, you could be influenced, even rip people off, but if you copied a band's sound, you were immediately fucking burned. More and more, as people started getting into it, you had the Black Flag clone bands, the Bad Religion clone bands, it got to the point where it all conformed, to this is the way it is, this is the way you should sound...

No deviating?

Jack: Yeah. No deviating. And those were the people didn't know what was going on anyway. It was a joke.

Why was anger and violence such an inherent part of punk?

Jack: A lot of people were pissed off, pissed off with no outlet. I know for us, a lot of us, a lot of people hit us up for being jocks or whatever, we were like sportsmen, we're all big guys.

All over six feet tall.

Jack: Yeah, we used to joke that we were the biggest band in the United States because everybody in the band averaged like six foot something.

But you also painted your face white and did un-jock things?

Jack: We all came from broken families and dealings with the police and school, and then you start looking different, so everywhere you go you're getting shit, and we were big enough to say, "Fuck you. You're not going to yell at me for having pink hair, or you'll get a crowbar across the face." That's how a lot of that went.

Critics say the first wave of LA punks like the Avengers, Dils, and Zeroes used violence as a metaphor, whereas as the beachcore and hardcore scene developed, the violence was tangible and physical.

Jack: I'll second it, cause none of those guys were going to use real violence. With a lot of the early arty bands, they were arty guys...

But when you reformed to play the Santa Monica gallery show, you teamed up with the arty bands, like the Bags, Urinals, and Zeros.

Jack: We loved them, but those weren't the kind of guys who were going to get in a Sunday football game with their friends. When it trickled out to the beach stuff, that's what it was. A bunch of athletes...

And rednecks?

Jack: No. A lot of the surfers were punk kids.

Ron: Surfers, skaters.

Jack: They were guys in shape. If you look at the early surf history of the 1950s and 60s, they were punks before there was punk, driving around with swastikas on their woodies, being fucked, you know. So, when it got down to us...

Huntington Beach, right?

Jack: And Long Beach, Venice, Hermosa, I mean these were the guys who were out in the sun all day, in good shape ... These were people who were getting into drunken fights anyway. We were hippies and liked to get into drunken fights. It was just one of things.

You were the first West Coast phenomena and could play shows up to 3,000 people at the Olympic, but has that all been eclipsed by bands

like Green Day? Will it remain an important part of punk history?

Jack: No, a lot of people don't know and don't care. People think that punk rock in L.A. was Black Flag with Henry, and that actually was the end of Black Flag. We had seen them with Keith Morris and shit, and it was like a whole different deal, like with Dez. I remember Gibby from the Butthole Surfers going, "How much did you make at that show?" cause he was shitting. I mean, we were getting paid a crazy amount of money back then. We were getting four-to-six thousand bucks a show. Back then, that was a fucking lot of money for a punk band.

Ron: But we paid countless shows for 25 bucks.

Jack: Yeah, but I'm talking about the sold out huge shows, when people were shitting and going, what the fuck? I mean all the bands on the bill got paid crazy. It was like hey, here's 500 bucks. There were baskets full of cash. It was pretty funny.

You've described yourself as an asshole kid with a high IQ? Is that still true, and how do you view you're pre-teen daughter?

Jack: My IQ is steadily lowering everyday. Actually, she's really cool about it. She's been around and seen it all. So she has a pretty straight head about all that stuff. I just took her to her first show a couple of weeks ago, and we were duct taping some chick to a chair, and my daughter was just like sitting there checking it out. I was like, "Don't do this at school" (laughs). Sometimes when the dad's fucked up, the kids come out a lot straighter. You know how straight parents sometimes get really fucked up kids? Out of fucked-up parents you get really straight kids.

Do you think parents who grew up around punk rock are any different than the baby boomer generation parents?

Jack: Yeah, I think my kid's a little more cynical. It's like they look at governments differently, they look at ads differently because I'm constantly on her about stuff. I mean, I wasn't raised like that. None of that shit even got mentioned at my house.

What happened in the late-1970s that turned your attention to punk rock?

Jack: There were a couple of things I was stoked on, well, like just meeting guys that caused trouble. That's how I met our drummer. I was causing all this shit at school, and this girl said, hey you should meet these guys, they're just like you. So I went over and met these guys.

Ron: Hellraisers!

Jack: We hug out, we talked about music, then we said, hey, we should start a band. So, we ripped her off that day, took a guitar, and started a band that day. I got into (it) mainly for the trouble and then later on (got) into the music.

What about you Ron?

Ron: I don't know what got me into it. I wasn't really into music, ever. I was into surfing and skating, that's it. Then sometime in 1978 the Dickies and Weirdos played a couple blocks from my house, and there were Elvis Costello and Joe Jackson, like we were mentioning. There were all these bands, and I kept going to shows. It seemed like every weekend you were going somewhere. And standing there watching these guys, I thought, I could do that. I worked a job in a parking lot until I could buy a guitar, then I quit. I bought my first guitar and just tried to do what they did. And I was really involved in the skate scene back then, so Steve Olson and I started our first band and toured skate parks and played with Jack and Todd's first band. Then it just came together.

Over the years, people have said that rock n roll is sometimes the only way that a poor or working class kid can stand up be counted, can be noticed.

Jack: That's nothing we ever thought about. We were clueless about that shit. It was never like, we're going to do this and be a success, it's just what we did. We played music. I was so fucking naïve about music. I was clueless. I thought everybody that got together and made a band that people liked, a ton of records sold, and everybody would come and see us (laughs). I had no other frame of reference. Like that was just the way it was. It wasn't like, yeah we're going to get out of the gutter or whatever. It was just like, this is what we do.

Do you think the three records you made with the Joykiller will be

remembered as being as powerful as your TSOL records, or will they slip to the backburner?

Jack: I don't know. I get a lot of good stuff from the Joykiller stuff. Especially the Static record, which Flipside voted record of the year. We had great reviews. At the time, we were doing something different. It was a time for us. It's real cool when people later on say, "Man, Beneath the Shadows was a great record, what a groundbreaking record." You guys did this and this, but that's never been what we're looking for. It's never been something we've looked for.

Do you think that anger or hostility is a creative force?

Jack: Yeah, a little bit, but we're anti-violent. I mean, we are so far fucking against it. It's not funny. We won't play backdrop music to it. If someone starts fighting, we stop.

Except you'll duct tape someone to a chair? (laughs)

Jack: But it's controlled mayhem. (laughs)

Do you think it's because you are older and more sober, you can control the chaos more than before?

Jack: The live shows are still pretty fucking full of chaos. I was telling some guy before, with this group of people, you take fire and a match, and it's always going to make a bad deal. No matter whether it's twenty years ago, it doesn't change those elements, fire and a match are still going to cause an explosion. It's the same thing we have now. It's like you stuck the fire and match together again twenty years later, there's fighting, fucking insanity, all that shit, nothing has changed. It's just that we're a bit older.

What's the least satisfying part about reforming and playing all these shows the past few years?

Jack: Getting harassed for using the name, that's one. Then, for me, getting yelled shit at, like play L.A. Guns, guys making rock comments, that pisses me off. The people getting confused about the fact that it was two completely different bands. Mainly, that's the shit. It's not about not getting paid for shows, long trips without money because that's been a factor always, that's never been it. It's the people yelling out the later songs or giving us shit. I remember a girl showing up at a Joykiller show with a Strange Love T-shirt on with a big fucking wig trying to burn us. That pissed me off. The rest of the stuff doesn't. We've always been underdogs. We're getting sued. We're being told we can't use our name.

On a very personal level, how has the way you see your music changed?

Jack: Musically, it's about the same. Basically, what's going on is the attitude is the same. The attitude we had then is the attitude we have now. We've always been libertarians: that's our badge. We're not anti-policemen, but we're anti-police. Our attitude has basically stayed the same: there's no back stage area, everyone's involved, you're not coming to see some rock stars, you're coming to see your friends play, get involved, you can do this too. We've always kept that same attitude no matter what. That's why people go and see shows and say, fuck, nothing has changed. There were reviews on the Warped tour saying how amazing the gap is between the old punks and the new punks. After seeing on the Warped tour, they were amazed to see how far the gap really was.

What constitutes the gap between you and Blink 182?

Jack: I can't say. I can't tell because we're doing it.

It's a studied routine for them, but you're still bringing something fresh to it?

Jack: Right. People were looking at us while we toured and saying, how the fuck do you do it? There's that sense of, well, this comes from people who have told me because I can never tell, but they say sometimes when they look at us, feel threatened. It's a scary situation, like, what might happen? I might get injured here ... You know, the fight or flight thing that kicks in at those shows because it's not a safe nice thing.

Isn't that what drew people to punk rock to begin with?

Jack: That's why I go. I used to joke with the kids, I'd have somebody doing a pulse check, you know that thing in Silence of the Lambs when they say, he ate her liver and his pulse didn't go above 80 (laughs).

That's what happens at these shows because unless some kid is going by me on fire, my pulse isn't above 62. We were at this show at the Troubador, and there was this little girl, the daughter of one of the guys from the Weirdos, who was sitting in front of the stage. There was all this craziness, this guy climbing up the light rack...

I heard you were egging kids to jump off the PA speakers.

Of course. (laughs) Every few minutes, I'd reach in and go, pulse check, to the girl, and she'd go there and do it and say, nah, it's still 60.

JACK GRISHAM POET WITH A HEART OF BEDLAM

Jack Grisham, singer of beach boys gone berserk TSOL, is a tour-de-force of American punk history still operating in full-bore style. His new memoir, *An American Demon*, which surveys his cataclysmic youth and early career, is not for the timid and meek. Like a meld of Oscar Wilde's *Dorian Gray* with *Fight Club* and *A Clockwork Orange*, he offers a savage poetry with an undertow of wit. In his lens, not-so-quiet Los Angeles suburbs become awash with dysfunction, revolt, and violence. Yet, in the end he offers a sense of recovery as well, a way to transcend personal chaos and find solace in the lurking memories.

Previously published by Houston Press, 2011

Although you are a demon, you are one damn literate demon, dropping references from Salome to Edgar Allen Poe. Is that your way of attacking -- using the cloak of literature?

I'm not sure if attack is the right word here. I use references that I hope the reader will be familiar with—mining fields of emotion that have been planted for hundreds of years. The use of a known past makes a future horror more believable.

Like Henry Miller and Rabelais, your book invokes poetry and ugliness, brutality and wisdom. Did you ever scare yourself when writing it?

It's terrifying to look at a self that is somewhat on the edge of reality, as if my unwillingness to see the truth somehow negated it. It was hard to sleep or to think of anything else other than the writing. I was obsessed and started to believe the worst of myself. Had I really created the world around me, and was I ultimately damned for what I'd been, and had done?

Most punks from the early era seem to have more emotional scars than tattoos. How did the memoir free you to be candid in ways that potent lyrics could not?

I wrote from outside myself, a passenger above my body as I tore through the lives of others—I could taste the blood, and yet the emotions were beneath me. My girlfriend, who pre-edited every line before it went to the publisher, would cry and beg me to stop. I attacked her for her unwillingness to discard her humanity. In the beginning, punk attracted the fringe, the cast-offs, and the supposedly unloved. I was adored by the kids around me, but for whatever reason, I thought their love was a lie.

People have told me you bait people, to reveal their biases and stupidity, and defeat or unsettle them. Your book seems to re-affirm this, even as you were a tiny kid. Do you ever regret it?

I've never regretted bringing down those that feed on the weak because their cowardice makes them easy targets. I'm a lazy attacker.

2001

HOUSTON 2011

INTERVIEW WITH JACK GRISHAM
FROM ARTCORE FANZINE ISSUE 24 SUMMER 2007

Love 'em or loathe 'em, T.S.O.L. have endured, in one form or another, throughout the years. From their early beginnings at the epicentre of the embryonic Southern Californian hardcore revolt, through their various experimentations with the punk rock form. An appearance in the cult punk flick 'Suburbia'. Dealings with countless record labels (Posh Boy, Frontier, Alternative Tentacles...) An ugly coup d'état by a new front man followed by a scouring of the depths of glam rock, culminating in the 'band' having no original members. Their subsequent reformation, and untimely death of their drummer Todd Barnes, followed by two albums of brand new material, before a shooting at a gig landed them in court and legal debt. Recently Jack Grisham's fellow stalwarts Ron Emory and Mike Roche moved away seeing the band play two farewell gigs before their latest hiatus. I fired a very helpful Jack Grisham a few questions...

WELLY - So you're having two great 'going away' gigs as Mike and Ron are moving out-of-state, is this really the end of T.S.O.L.? If not, how do you foresee things working in the future?

JACK - It's not really the "end" of TSOL because if we say that Joe Wood and the boys will be out next week with a new "T.S.O.L." disc. We are just taking a break for awhile... a long while.

WELLY - Where do you stand now financially after being embroiled in the court case over the shooting at one your gigs? Has this played any role in the way things have been going for the band?

JACK - Broke as always.

WELLY - A few of us here in the U.K. have been disappointed after two aborted tours. What caused the cancellations, and what are the chances now of you ever visiting these climes?

JACK - Our families are more important than touring and we are obligated towards them. You hear a lot of these punks bitching about the government and corporate bullshit but these same people are not willing to enact change in the one place they can, their own homes. We treat our families with respect and love and so anything that might interfere with that comes second. I was in Germany one time and my daughter had a crisis at home, we were on the phone and she was crying and needing me there but I was off being a "rock star". It was then that I realized that she was what meant the most to me.

WELLY - Your interview on the American Hardcore movie seem to already be causing controversy following your comments about being a 'rapist' and 'grave-robbing' and the like. Did you actually do all that stuff or were you just going for shock value?

JACK - Not for shock value. At times I could be a real evil vicious fuck and I am not proud of it. Years of just pleasing myself can inflate an ego to the point of unbelief.

WELLY - How did it feel to rejoin the band after everything that happened during the 'dark years' and release two albums of new material. Did you feel vindicated? How did you manage to bury the hatchet with the other original members? And what about Joe Wood, seeing as he is your brother-in-law?

JACK - Did have a lot of resentment towards them and there has been quite a bit of hard feelings to be overcome so I constantly remind them about what cunts they are!

WELLY - From the outset you changed the approach and sound on each T.S.O.L. release. If you had to pick one favourite era and style, which would it be and why?

JACK - Don't know if I have a favourite it was just something we had to do. Punk rock was suppose to be open-minded and fun so I tried to make it that.

WELLY - Most bands from your era and area got some pretty raw deals with record labels. Which stand out as the best and worst labels that you've dealt with throughout your history? Do you actually own the rights to any of your material?

JACK - No we don't own any of it and I refuse to comment so I don't lose what little they send me.

WELLY - What made you decide to run for governor of California? What did you learn from the experience? And did you rub shoulders with any strange people or kiss any babies?

JACK - I did it mainly to bitch about health care. We've got a government over here that is constantly telling the world how great America is, and then they turn around and not take care of their own people. The medical community in America is flush with greed and keeping us sick keeps money in their pockets. The majority of Americans cannot afford health care and the quality of the care they can afford is poor at best. The coolest thing about running for office was the opportunity it gave me to go to the primary schools and teach the children about how to get involved and to confirm the fact that they do matter and that they do not have to sit by while their communities and families are being lied to and destroyed.

WELLY - You started out as a band with political lyrics, but soon changed for a different approach. In light of your political campaign, did you remain politically motivated over the years? If so, why did you decide not to continue exploring it lyrically?

JACK - How many times can you say fuck the government before it becomes such a common phrase that it loses all power? A lot of these bands now a days have no idea what there even "rebelling" against.

WELLY - What does a punk rock legend do when not touring or running for office? Flipping burgers or cashing royalty cheques?

JACK - Wish I was cashing checks, I spend the majority of my time with family and friends and I am heavily involved with helping sufferers of alcohol and drug addiction get help. You see I didn't say crusading against alcohol and drugs because I don't have anything against those things I just make sure I'm available when they start taking over peoples lives.

WELLY - How does it feel now making ends meet and seeing bands influenced by T.S.O.L. enjoy commercial success like your Offpsrings, AFIs and Alkaline Trios of this world.

JACK - The one thing good about not having money is you know people are not "respecting" you and "loving" you for your dough, because you don't have any!

WELLY - It's the old desert island discs question. Which five albums can you not live without, and why?

JACK - In no real order: Machine Gun Etiquette by the Damned (best rock record ever!) Revolver by the Beatles. Were only in it for the money by Frank Zappa and the Mothers of Invention. Chet Baker sings by Chet Baker. Euphoric Recall by The Kuehn and Jones Orchestra.

WELLY - Which springs to mind as the craziest gig you ever played or attended? What did you think when you suggested the audience sit down before the cops stormed the gig at SIR Studios, and everyone actually did?

JACK - Too many crazy gigs to pull out just one but the S.I.R studio thing was a little wild. I wasn't like on a power trip or anything we were just real connected and it was like making a suggestion to a friend "let's sit down and fuck with the cops" and they just did it. 3,000 people sitting on the floor was pretty nice though.

WELLY - What for you, is the most glaring difference between punk rock of old and the present day?

JACK - Lack of commitment.

WELLY - What do you have planned musically or personally now that T.S.O.L. will be on the back burner, and what other amusing meanings for the initials T.S.O.L. have you come up with over the years?

JACK - I'm working on a real mellow disc and band called the Kuehn and Jones Orchestra with Greg Kuehn from TSOL. its fun just to switch gears and watch people spin.

JACK GRISHAM ON... [FROM ARTCORE]

THE FIRST 12"

"Recorded in an afternoon for 500 dollars. The vocals were done in the studio bathroom and if you listen very close you can hear a motorcycle go by. The contract for this record was such shit, we flushed it down a hotel toilet."

DANCE WITH ME

"Recorded in two days for 1200 dollars. ripped off again, and if there is a hell Lisa Fancher is going to be there. Although I can't really blame her because we were stupid drunk kids who would have signed anything for beer money and a new surfboard. People said we'd switched to Goth rock on this one, but it's such shit because we had all these songs before we did the first EP."

WEATHERED STATUES

"Never played these songs before the studio takes. the laughing in 'Man and Machine' was real because I was just fucking around and we kept the first take."

BENEATH THE SHADOWS

"A bit hard to listen to cause I sing it so badly, but this record was great to make. Five straight days and if we felt like doing it we did it. The goal in TSOL was to never repeat ourselves and this was no exception."

LIVE '91

"Actually recorded in '89... live my ass. All the vocals had to be redone because all you heard was people yelling fuck into the mic."

DISAPPEAR

"Some good songs but poor execution, we were just getting back together and learning to write together again. I'm just glad we were able to finish it without killing each other."

DIVIDED WE STAND

"My favourite TSOL record... had fun recording it and live the songs were great to play."

WHO'S SCREWIN' WHO?

"Exactly what it says. Re-recording our own songs to control the rights."

2012

BIJAN OSKOUIE

A FAN TRIBUTE

I first met Jack in 1996 at Emo's in Houston, Texas. He was on tour with the Joykiller for Static, their second album. I had heard TSOL years ago in skate videos and had enjoyed what I'd heard. I don't recall how I found the Joykiller, but after listening to the music and the lyrics, I was immediately a fan. I hung out after the show that night, which was killer, and spoke to Jack for a bit. I got his number, and we stayed in touch. I have a Static T-Shirt, which I am sure Jack must've given me back then because financial insecurity was a way of life for me at that time.

Fast forward a year or so and I caught the Joykiller at Fitzgerald's in Houston for the tour supporting Three, their third album. We caught up. By this time, TSOL had come up in conversation, either by me or by someone else while I was nearby. My impression was that it was a non-issue, for it just wasn't a realistic proposition.

So, imagine my surprise, in 1999, to hear that the band had reformed. I was stoked, as this was quite a surprise, given what I had heard in the past. I believe the Social Chaos tour rolled through Houston in (I believe) October of 1999. I also met Ron Emory and Mike Roche at that time, and we all hung out a little bit before and after the show. If my memory serves me correctly, this was the show that a kid broke one of the windows of the band's vehicle. The kid was caught, and Jack denied him an ass whipping, instead giving a lecture about honor and other things I can't remember. I DO remember that it was way more entertaining that seeing someone get beat up.

The next year I flew into L.A. to stay with Ron and see everyone else. Ron's girlfriend (now wife) Gia was supposed to pick me up from LAX. Ron said, "Look for an attractive redhead." So, I was walking around LAX asking every redhead, "Are you Gia?" I had gone through this two times already. On my third pass through the terminal, I decided I'd catch a cab to Marina Del Ray if I struck out again. Well, I struck out, and was a bit unhappy. Imagine my surprise when, upon exiting the terminal, there's Jack and Bobby rolling up to pick me up. I have never forgotten this gesture, as picking someone up from the airport is just below helping someone move. Coincidentally, the band was recording Disappear, their first record since reforming. I got to spend time at the studio for a few days while they worked, which was extremely cool. I do have some great video of them playing at Sam's Seafood in Seal Beach. Jack's shenanigans cut that show WAY short. Venue owners don't take it kindly when you hold a lighter up to thatched decorations and mention a scene in a movie where a restaurant is torched. But that's Jack -- he's easily one of the best frontmen I've ever seen, and one of the best shit talkers ever.

I came out the next year and drove down from L.A. to Huntington Beach to see Jack. The Adolescents were playing that night at the Galaxy for a reunion of The Blue Album, and we went. You know what, I could sit here and type plenty of other stories along these lines, but screw that. Yeah, I'm a huge fan of Jack's musical output, but that's not why I'm writing this.

But even if Jack quit making music when the Joykiller split up, I'd still wanna hang out with him. You'll read in here how Jack can't stand the elitism that ironically exists in Punk Rock today. To him, that's not just something he says, it's something he lives. He has always made me feel welcome to hang out and be a part of, and I mean BIG TIME. Once, while traveling with TSOL through Texas, somewhere on I-35 between Dallas and Austin, in the middle of a very cold night, he turns to me and says: "Bijan, you wanna drive for a bit?" Now, this is a large RV with a trailer. My response was something along the lines of, "Oh, hell no." But again, that's Jack -- he is extremely generous and pretty damn transparent.

Here is something that always sticks with me, and it says a lot about what kind of man Jack has become. So, last summer, TSOL was on the Warped Tour. Not my idea of a good time, but I'm not going to NOT go see my friends. So, I went to the hotel the day before and gave Jack a ride. He said thanks, and I said something along the lines of: "Dude - you picked me up from LAX years ago; I owe you." He didn't recall doing that, and I have a really good idea of why. Here's why: he's done that kind of thing for all kinds of people, not just me, and he can't retain ALL of that info. Yeah, you'll read in these pages examples of Jack at his lowest, or some of the bad things he's done. But he won't brag about the good he's done, about the joy his company and stories bring to people, or about his naked honesty about his humanity that helps people in a way that words just don't do justice.

I'm not special. I'm sure people all over the world have had similar experiences with Jack. I admire the shit out of Jack (and, I gotta say, Ron and Mike). I am always reminded of ways I can be a better person after time spent with them.

I've known Jack for 22 years, and those 22 years are better because of that. That includes music, but I have SO many great memories that don't revolve around that: they just revolve around having fun.

TSOL 2002 BY BIJAN OSKOUIE

CONCERT FACTORY

FRI, APR. 6	**TSOL**
SAT, APR. 7	**45 GRAVE**
SAT, APR. 9	**CRAMPS VAND**
	SHATTERED FA
THURS, APR. 12	Germanys Metal Invades **BALLS TO THE W.**
SUN, APR. 15	**HEAVY PETT**
WED, APR. 18	**DICKIES**
THURS, APR. 19	**LOS ILLEGA**
SAT, APR. 21	**ALCATRAZZ**

GOVERNMENT ISSUE

TRUE SOUL OF LIBER

MARGIN MAN

Fri. Nov 9
Wilson Center

8 pm

T. S. O.
ALL AGES
THRS. MAR. 1

FITZLIVE.COM

FITZGERALD'S
2706 White Oak @ Studemont   713-862-3838

MAU-MAU

BEAUTY ONLY

T·S·O·L·

FLIPPER

AK-47

WOLF & RISSMILLER'S
Country Clu
20 FT VIDEO PROJECTION
Tickets at BOX OFFICE, TICKETRON, TICKETCHARGE (21
and CHARGE-LINE. Concert Information Line 881
Ventura Freeway to Reseda Exit, North to Sherm
18415 SHERMAN WAY RESEDA (213) 881-9

e u.s. war in el salvador

SALVADOR

To do so, U.S. officials insist, would be to hand the 23 million people of Guatemala, El Salvador, Honduras, Nicaragua, Costa Rica, Panama and Belize over to the oppression of communism and put the vital interests of the United States in peril.

Farabundo Marti National Liberation Front guerrillas and their political allies in the FDR

MAY 12   9 P.M.
ADVANCE
AT THE DOOR

T.S.O.L.

AUG18

FITZGERALD'S

706 White Oak @ Studemont 713-862-3838

5 KNAC & RODENT
PRESENTS
t.s.o.l.

TIX ON SALE 12-1

OCIAL
DISTORTION

RBAL ABUSE

RED ALERT
& OTIS

EMBER 31   8:00 P

ROADWAY THEATER

ETS AVAILABLE AT ZED RECO
AH'S, VINLY FETTISH, CAMEL SIG

T.S.O.L.

TRUE SOUNDS OF LIBERTY FROM L

★ BIG BOYS ★

NOV. 20 .DALLAS. HOT KLUB

ew Movie...

SUBURBIA

About A New Generation.

A Roger Corman-Bert Dragin Production

Kids CHRIS PEDERSON BILL COYNE JENNIFER CLAY and ANDREW PECE

cert performances by T.S.O.L. THE VANDALS DI Music by ALEX GIBSON

Director of Photography TIMOTHY SUHRSTEDT Editor ROSS ALBERT

duced by BERT DRAGIN Written and Directed by PENELOPE SPHEERIS

TARTS AUG. 3

ROXY

SCREENING ROOMS I & II
2021-23 SANSOM   561-0114

WILD IN THE STREETS: L.A. PUNK

MUSIC SO

HAVE YOU HEARD ABOUT SHERRY?

TSOL
THE DICKIES
D.I.
CHANNEL 3

...day, June 18
7 to 11 pm

Museum of the American West
4700 Western Heritage Way
Los Angeles, CA 90027

www.museumoftheamericanwest.org

www.ticketweb.com.

...ets: $15 ($8 for Autry National Center members). For tickets call TicketWeb at 866.468.3399, or visit www.ticketweb.com.

Sponsored in part by Amoeba Music

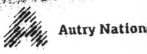

Autry Nation

...compliments of Raymond Pettibon

Alucard Productions present

URBAN STRUGGLE:
he battle of the Cuckoo's Nest

Featuring Performances by:

BLACK FLAG · CIRCLE JERKS
T.S.O.L.
Theme song by:
The VANDALS

Photographs by Ed Colver and Glen E. Friedman
Produced by Jerry Roach and Paul Young

emiering Thursday, December 29th

at the Surf Theater in Huntington Beach
located at the corner of 5th St. and Pacific Coast Highway.
For more information call (714) 536-9396

STATE
theatre
original members
T.S.O.L
THE JACKIE PAPERS
PSUEDO HEROES
AUGUST 15th - SUNDA
TICKETS $8.00 - DOORS 8:00 p.
687 Central Ave
St. Petersburg
INFO. (727) 895-3045
TICKETMASTER www.ticketma
· select SPEC'S
select PUBLIX SUPER MARKETS
(813) 287-8844 · (813) 898-210

GOVERNMENT ISSUE
TSOL
Naked Raygun

Cereal Killer

JUNE 20, '85

GIVE US STABB OR GIVE US DEATH

WUST RADIO HALL
8th & 'V', N.W., Washington, D.C.

$6 Tix at Y&T, Rec.& Tape,

OST Productions

BAD RELIGIO

Tickets for the North Hollywood Theater and the Whisky will be

L.O.S.T.

Featuring the original members doing the
JACK GRISHAM   **MIKE ROCHE**
RON EMORY   **TODD BA**

and **INSTED**

HOLLYWOOD PALLADIUM   **FRIDAY, FEBRUARY 1**

TICKETMASTER (213)480-3232   **MUSIC PLUS**   **MAY C**

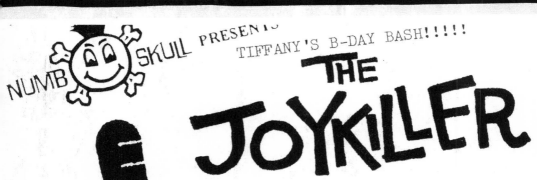

NUMB SKULL PRESENTS

TIFFANY'S B-DAY BASH!!!!!

THE JOYKILLER

EPITAPH

SKiNNY ROGE

DiCK CiRCU

I FEEL LIKE THE GIRL WITH THE MOST CAKE!

ALL AGES $6

TUESDAY, AUGUST 8, 8P
COLUMBUS HALL 36 South Figu
downtown Ventura   corner of Figueroa/Santa Cla

Sat. June 1

athedral of Tears

DIN

DETONATORS

THE HAGS

A.T.G

SINCERE FIBERS

photo/William Franklin McMahon

SCRATCH
BONGOWAX
THE SUPERKOOLS
HIT 36
TENDER FURY

TURDAY JUNE 6, 92

RAJI'S

O HOLLYWOOD BLVD.

0:00

OVER

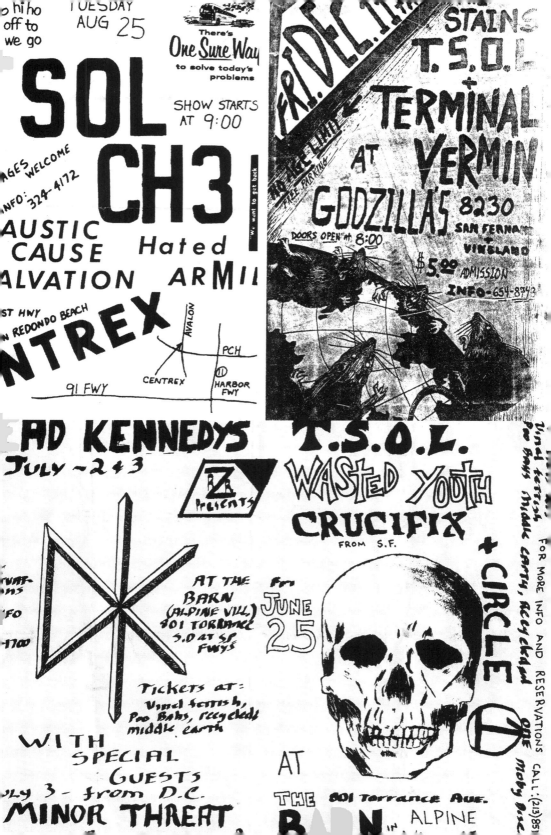

hi ho
off to
we go

TUESDAY AUG 25

There's
One Sure Way
to solve today's
problems

SHOW STARTS
AT 9:00

SOL

AGES WELCOME
INFO: 324-4172

CH3

AUSTIC
CAUSE   Hated
ALVATION   ARMII

We want to get back

ST HWY
N REDONDO BEACH

NTREX

AVALON
PCH
91 FWY   CENTREX   HARBOR
FWY

FRI. DEC. 11

STAINS
T.S.O.L.
+
TERMINAL
AT **VERMIN**
GODZILLAS 8230
SAN FERNAN
+
VINELAND
DOORS OPEN at 8:00
$5.00 ADMISSION
INFO-654-8792

AD KENNEDYS
JULY ~ 2+3

Z PRESENTS

T.S.O.L.
WASTED YOUTH
CRUCIFIX
FROM S.F.

AT THE
BARN
(ALPINE VILL)
901 TORRANCE
S.D AT SF
FWYS

Tickets at:
Vinyl fettish,
Poo Bahs, recycled,
middle earth

WITH
SPECIAL
GUESTS
LY 3 - from D.C.
MINOR THREAT

Fri
JUNE
25

+ CIRCLE

AT

THE
BARN
901 Torrance Ave.
ALPINE
N. IN

Vinyl fettish, FOR MORE INFO AND
Poo Bahs, middle earth, recycled
RESERVATIONS
ONE
CALL:(213)85
Moby Disc

JACK GRISHAM
OF
TSOL

CACTUS Free **MUSIC**
ALL **AGES**

PUNK discussion

THE ORIGINAL MEMBERS
TSOL
JACK
MIKE
RON
TODD
FRI.
DEC. 29
CELEBRITY THEAT
201 E. BROADWAY, 1/2 BLOCK EAST OF ANAH
LOCATIONS, MAY CO., MUS
(213) 480-3232 • (714) 740-2
TICKETMASTER

THE NERVE AGENTS

ON TOUR NOW!!!   AUG 18
W/ T.S.O.L.   FITZ

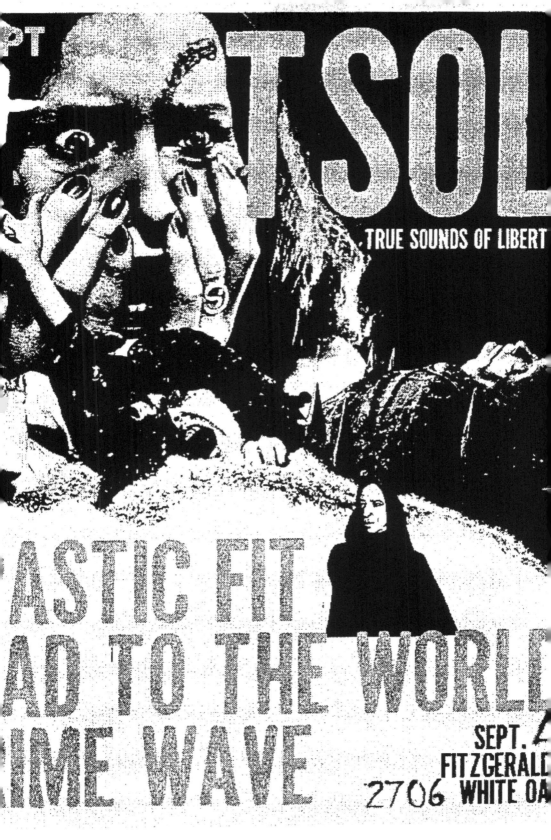

T.S.O.L. T.S.O.L. T.S.O.L. T.S.O.L. T.S.O.L. T.S.O.L. T.S.O.L. T.

MINORITIES WELCOME

SEE THE TRUE SOUNDS OF LIBERTY AT THE CU - koos NEST NOV.
SEE THE SCREWZ
SEE THE ARISTOCATS

BRING FALSE IDENTIFICATION

T.S.O.L. EAT GOOD

ENRAGED BY A SPANKING ,AN 11-year-old SHOVES HIS MOTHER
AGAINST A DOORJAM FRACTURING HER BACK. WHEN SHE FALLS,
HE KICKS HER IN THE FACE

NOVEMBER 18 CUKOOS NEST NOVEMBER 18. NOVEMBER 18 CUKOOS NEST

Q: ARE WE NOT HUMAN BEINGS?
A: NO, WE ARE SHEEP!

ow long are you going to let the goverment push you around? High
police oppression, shipping our children to schools they don't want
tend, and the constant threat of TOTAL NUCLEAR DESTRUCTION? TOO LONG!!!
rment for and by the people has turned to a mockery for and by the rich.
GOVERMENT, DESTROY POWER, LIVE YOUR LIFE AS YOU SEE FIT! You need freedom
ve and love as we choose. Freedom to survive in our present world.
T.S.O.L. is an organization formed to warn the people of a corrupt
ment. Take the time to think of your future. All young men 18-20, are
eady to fight and die for a country who screws you yearly with the I.R.S.?
sn't important enough to die or kill for. ALL races and ages must join
her for peace. FUCK FACISM, FUCK RACISM, AND FUCK THE SYSTEM! ALL men
reated equal under the laws of our country, but some are more equal than
s. If you love your country, your family, and yourself, then save them all,
up silent majority! Go see the TRUE SOUNDS OF LIBERTY and change the
tion we're heading, from Nuclear Destruction to PEACE!

A Hell Of A Way To Treat Heroes!

Come SEE
THE
ADOLECENTS
AND
T.S.O.L
aT THE FAB
CUKOOS NEST
FRIDAY NIGHT
MARCH 6th
AT 7:00 P.M

DUG YOUR GRAVE
NOW JUMP IN IT!

T.S.O.L.

Out in March

on Alternative Tentacles /

4 Song EP   Faulty Products

2018

2015

2011

2001

2018

2012

2018

2012

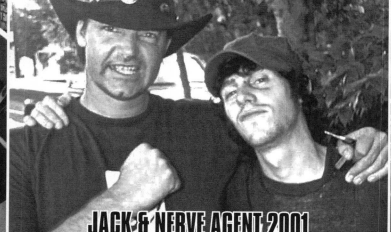

JACK CACTUS MUSIC HOUSTON 2001

JACK & NERVE AGENT 2001

TSOL 1982 BY KEVIN MURPHY

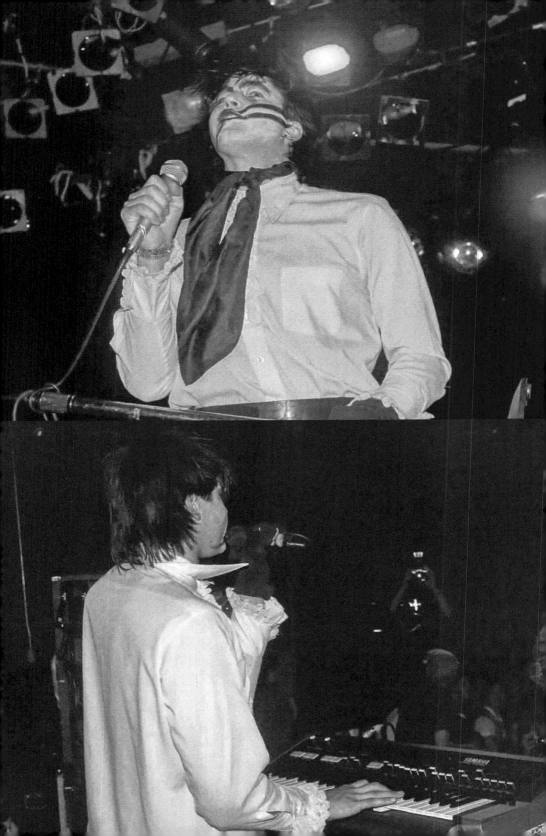

TSOL BY ED COLVER

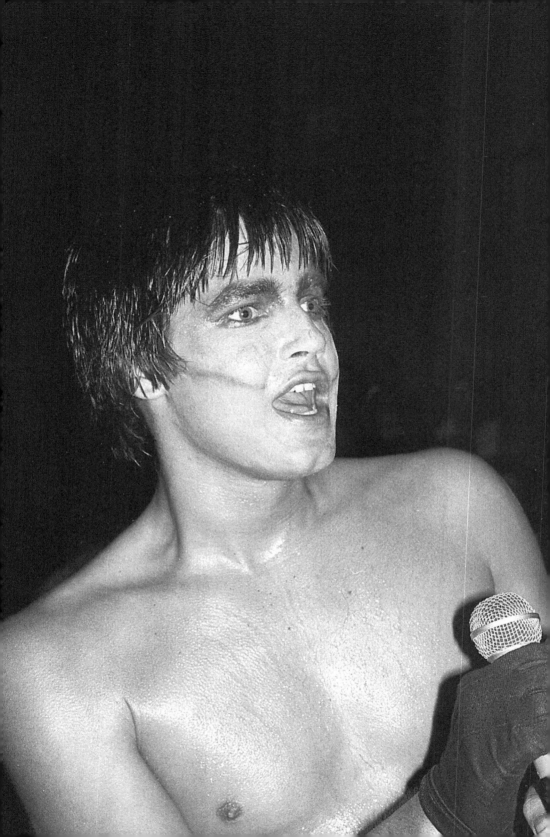

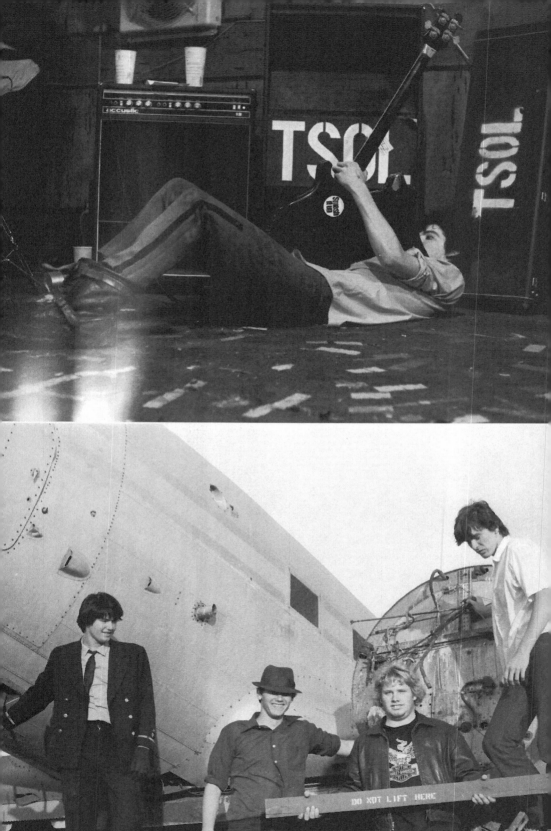

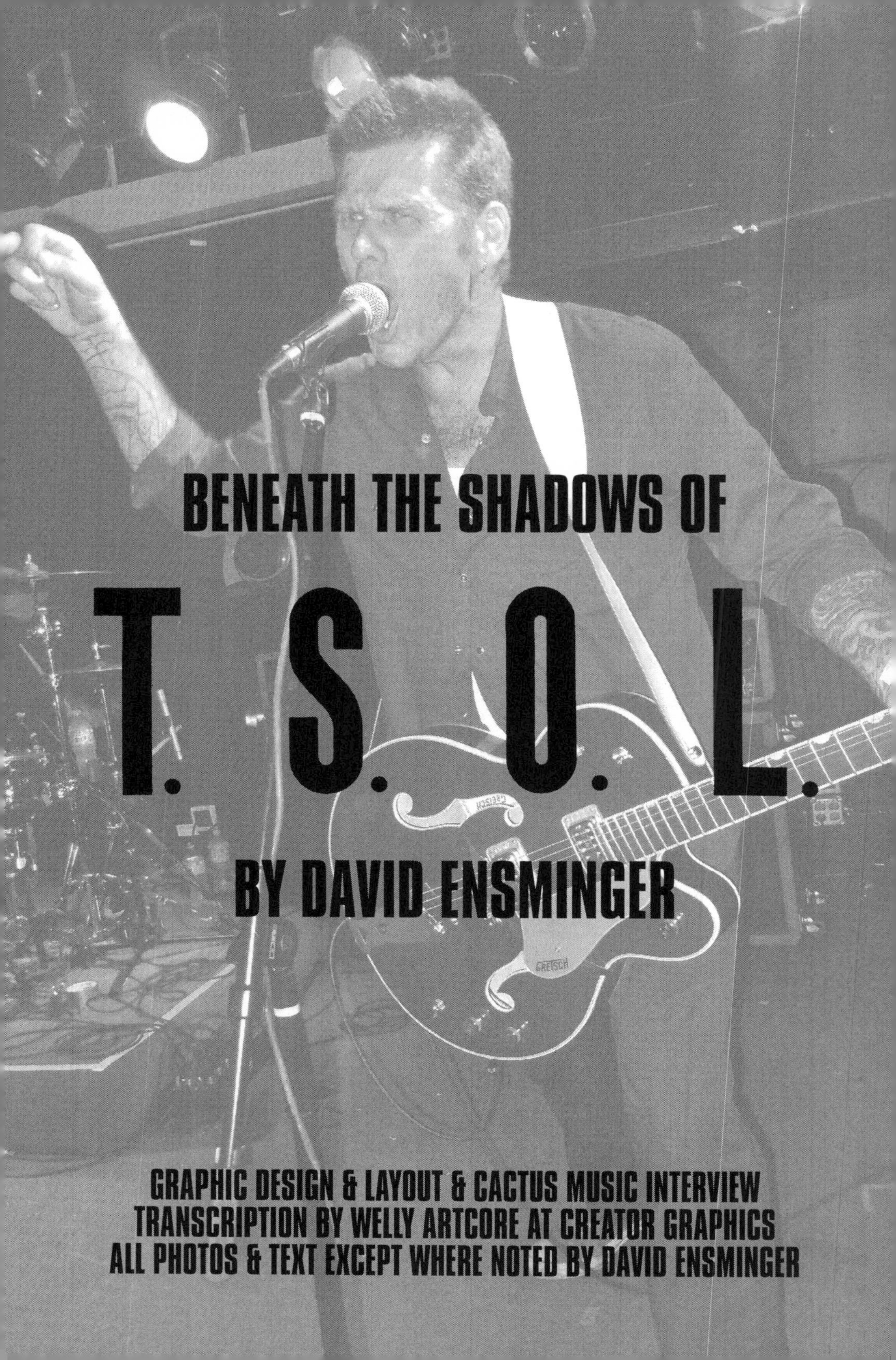

BENEATH THE SHADOWS OF

T. S. O. L.

BY DAVID ENSMINGER

GRAPHIC DESIGN & LAYOUT & CACTUS MUSIC INTERVIEW
TRANSCRIPTION BY WELLY ARTCORE AT CREATOR GRAPHICS
ALL PHOTOS & TEXT EXCEPT WHERE NOTED BY DAVID ENSMINGER

Made in the USA
Middletown, DE
11 August 2024

58932658R00076